Presented to

_____

By

_____

On the Occasion of

_____

Date

_____

WHEN I'M ON MY KNEES

Devotional Thoughts on Prayer for Women

ANITA CORRINE DONIHUE

BARBOUR BOOKS

An Imprint of Barbour Publishing, Inc.

Special thanks to my beloved husband, Bob, for his love, support, and inspiration.

Table of Contents

INTRODUCTION

"Well, all we can do is pray about it."

Oh, no! I can't believe I said that. Again. *All* we can do is pray? How short-sighted can I be? Great things happen while I'm on my knees. Forces of heaven are released when one person goes to prayer. The same power that raised my Lord Jesus from the dead is available for my needs.

Thank You that when I bow in prayer, Your Son intercedes. In His purity, He raises each of my petitions to You.

Help me pray within Your will. Guide me to right motives while I pray. Give me faith to release my prayers, to commit them to Your power, Your love, and Your glory.

Remind me often, Lord, that according to Your will, prayer can move mountains, stop rivers, form seasons, and, best of all, change hearts.

Father, here are my concerns and needs. I commit them to You. I thank You in Jesus' name for the answers that will come according to Your will. I trust Your wisdom and give You all the praise.

❑❑❑

And he who searches our hearts knows the mind of the Spirit, because the Spirit intercedes for the saints in accordance with God's will.

Romans 8:27, NIV

PART 1

PRAISE

JOYFUL, JOYFUL, WE ADORE THEE

Joyful, joyful, we adore Thee.
God of glory, Lord of love;
Hearts unfold like flowers before Thee,
Opening to the sun above.

Melt the clouds of sin and sadness,
Drive the dark of doubt away;
Giver of immortal gladness,
Fill us with the light of day.

Henry Van Dyke

❑❑❑

Give unto the Lord, O ye mighty,
give unto the Lord glory and strength.
Give unto the Lord the glory
due unto his name; worship the Lord
in the beauty of holiness.
Psalm 29:1–2, KJV

PRAISE YOU FOR YOUR PATIENCE

Father, thank You for being so patient with me. For the many times I mess things up and You are still there for me, I am grateful. You are truly my heavenly Father. How thankful I am for Your tender mercies, Your sympathy toward me when I need You most. I reverence You, Lord. How marvelous are Your wondrous ways, how kind Your forgiving grace.

When I'm not wise in my spending, You still provide my needs; when I stumble, You hold me up. You watch over me through day and night.

You protect me from harm's way, wrapping Your wings about me as an eagle protects her young. She carries them on her wings and doesn't let them fall. Thank You for carrying me, too.

Praise You for Your endless love and compassion. You have kept me safe from disaster so many times. You heal my illnesses. You strengthen my mind, soul, and body. Thank You for the love You show me every day.

Forgive me for my thoughtlessness and the times I mistreat You. I can't understand why You love me!

I marvel that You know me so well. You know the hairs on my head. You care about the pain in my head, my hands, my back, my feet. When a sparrow falls, You care. How much then You must care for me.

Help me, Father, to think before I act, to be more cautious, and to take better care of myself. Thank You for Your patience and forgiving love.

❑❑❑

Bless the Lord, O my soul: and all that is within me, bless his holy name. Bless the Lord, O my soul, and forget not all his benefits:

Who forgiveth all thine iniquities; who healeth all thy diseases;

Who redeemeth thy life from destruction; who crowneth thee with loving kindness and tender mercies;

Who satisfieth thy mouth with good things; so that thy youth is renewed like the eagle's.

The Lord executeth righteousness and judgment for all that are oppressed.

He made known his ways unto Moses, his acts unto the children of Israel.

The Lord is merciful and gracious, slow to anger, and plenteous in mercy.

He will not always chide: neither will he keep his anger for ever.

He hath not dealt with us after our sins; nor rewarded us according to our iniquities.

For as the heaven is high above the earth, so great is his mercy toward them that fear him.

As far as the east is from the west, so far hath he removed our transgressions from us.

Like as a father pitieth his children, so the Lord pitieth them that fear him.

Psalm 103:1–12, KJV

PATIENCE

Is there ambition in my heart?
Search, gracious God, and see;
Or do I act a haughty part?
Lord, I appeal to Thee.

I charge my thoughts, be humble still,
All my carriage mild,
Content, my Father, with Thy will,
And quiet as a child.

The patient soul, the lowly mind
Shall have a large reward:
Let saints in sorrow lie resign'd,
And trust a faithful Lord.

Isaac Watts

THANK YOU FOR PROVISION

Father, I praise You, for You know perfectly well each of my needs, even before I ask. Sometimes You know better than I. You love me so much that You gave Your only Son so I could be free from sin and You could adopt me as Your child. Because of this, I give You first place in my life, and I commit myself to living as You want me to.

Not only do You give me all I need, but You also provided this earth for us to live on; You control the beginning and end of all that lives; You have given me the present; and You lay out my future before me. Nothing really belongs to me, yet how You shower Your blessings upon me to enjoy.

Thank You, Lord, for being my Shepherd. Thank You for watching over and protecting me as a shepherd does his sheep.

I feel confident and unafraid as You direct me each day. When You provide for me, I find enough overflowing goodness to share with others. How blest I am to have You as my Savior!

You are unchanging. I can always depend on You. Thank You for Your faithfulness. Praise You for caring for me and my loved ones from one generation to the next, as we love You and obey Your Word.

I will not fear tomorrow for You take care of that, too. I try to prepare for the future, yet I live one day at a time, trusting You.

I lift my voice in praise to You. May my thoughts

and deeds give You great joy. Let my heart be pure and blameless in Your sight. I shall lift Your name in joyful song forever and ever.

❑❑❑

Sing to the Lord a new song;
   sing to the Lord, all the earth.
Sing to the Lord, praise his name;
   proclaim his salvation day after day.
Declare his glory among the nations,
   his marvelous deeds among all peoples.

For great is the Lord and most worthy of praise;
   he is to be feared above all gods.

Ascribe to the Lord, O families of nations,
   ascribe to the Lord glory and strength.
Ascribe to the Lord the glory due his name;
   bring an offering and come into his courts.
Worship the Lord in the splendor of his holiness;
   tremble before him, all the earth.

Psalm 96:1–4, 7–9, NIV

FREEDOM FROM SIN

I shudder at how I was once in sin's bondage, Lord Jesus. Then You saved me. All I had to do was ask You into my heart and You forgave my every single sin. How wonderful to be set free of all that horrible baggage I was carrying around in my life. How marvelous to enjoy fellowship with You. Thank You, Lord, for Your saving grace.

Although my life was a mess when I gave it to You, You loved me anyway. Step by step You performed miracles within me, like You did years ago for Paul when he was in prison. You broke my chains of sin and entrapment. You led me through every door of my life and helped me to mature in You.

How can You forgive me for my wrong doings? Over and over I slip. Over and over You catch me and stamp out the destructive rotten sins. I have difficulty even forgiving myself, but with Your mighty hand You cast my sins into the deepest sea. Help me, Lord, for only then am I free from sin.

How amazing, the way You freed me. I'm so much happier, my health even improves. You give me energy and life each day, life more abundant than ever.

Once I had no hope. I lived in utter confusion without direction or goals. My paths were like quicksand, ready to swallow me up into total darkness.

For so long I held back from giving my heart to You. I didn't want to lose control. Yet, when I was willing to let my will be crucified on the cross with

You, Lord, You began to live within me. You are my Deliverer and loving Friend. You have set my feet on a firm path, and I fear no more.

Thank You for how You love me and give of Yourself. How I praise You, Lord, for freedom from crippling sin. I'm so thankful Your death wasn't a lost cause. You have saved so many sinners such as I and given joy beyond measure.

Here in calm communion I seek Your guidance. Thank You for how You lead me along the right paths. Thank You for hearing me and helping each time I call upon Your name. I walk within Your strength. I praise You for how You wrap me in the garments of Your salvation and place the robe of righteousness about my shoulders.

I take joy in putting other things aside, for You are first in my life. No longer will I depend on my own good works, but instead on Your wonderful grace. Thanks be to You, God!

□□□

To the Jews who had believed him,
Jesus said, "If you hold to my teaching, you are
really my disciples. Then you will know the truth,
and the truth will set you free."
John 8:31–32, NIV

THE SAVIOUR

Behold the Saviour of mankind
Nailed to the shameful tree;
How vast the love that Him inclined
To bleed and die for me.

Hark! how He groans, while nature shakes,
And earth's strong pillars bend!
The Temple's veil asunder breaks,
The solid marbles rend.

'Tis finished! now the ransom's paid,
"Receive My Soul!" He cries;
See—How He bows His sacred head!
He bows His head and dies!

But soon He'll break death's iron chain,
And in full glory shine,
O Lamb of God! was ever pain—
Was ever love like Thine?

Samuel Wesley, Sr.

YEARS I SPENT IN VANITY AND PRIDE

Years I spend in vanity and pride,
Caring not my Lord was crucified,
Knowing not it was for me He died
On Calvary.

Now I've given to Jesus everything;
Now I gladly own Him as my King,
Now my raptured soul can only sing
Of Calvary.

O the love that drew salvation's plan!
O the grace that brought it down to man!
O the mighty gulf that God did span
At Calvary!

Mercy there was great, and grace was free;
Pardon there was multiplied to me;
There my burdened soul found liberty,
At Calvary.

William Reed Newell

Out of the depths have I cried unto thee, O Lord.

Lord, hear my voice; let thine ears be attentive to the voice of my supplications.

If thou, Lord, shouldest mark iniquities, O Lord, who shall stand?

But there is forgiveness with thee, that thou mayest be feared.

I wait for the Lord, my soul doth wait, and in his word do I hope.

Psalm 130:1–5, KJV

THANK YOU FOR YOUR HOLY SPIRIT

Thank You, Father, for Your wonderful Holy Spirit. Great and wondrous is Your presence. I feel Your warm love about me. You fill my heart with praise to You. You are so dear. I open my heart to Your Holy Spirit to nurture and lead me, for Your ways are just and true.

Because of Your love, Holy Spirit, I am learning to love others more. I strive to love them as much as You do me. Through all our imperfections, Your love helps make up for the many faults of others, as well as my own.

Holy Spirit, fill me daily. Groom me so I may produce the fruits of Your Spirit. Make my cup overflow so I may be a blessing to those around me.

Great and wondrous is Your presence. Your ways are just and true. Your comfort is with me day and night, everlasting to everlasting. How great You are!

❑❑❑

But the fruit of the Spirit is
love, joy, peace, patience, kindness, goodness,
faithfulness, gentleness, and self-control.
Against such things there is no law.
Galatians 5:22–23, NIV

PRAISE YOU FOR SPIRITUAL FRUIT

Love beyond measure
Selfless and free.
Joy in each moment
Comes only from Thee.

Peace, lasting peace
Through Your infinite love,
Patience and kindness
From Heaven above.

Goodness that's wrought by
Repentance and tears,
Faithfulness lasting
All through the years.

Gentleness laced with
Strong self-control,
To You, Holy Spirit,
I give heart and soul.

❏❏❏

But the Comforter,
which is the Holy Ghost,
whom the Father will send in my name,
he shall teach you all things,
and bring all things to your remembrance,
whatsoever I have said unto you.
John 14:26, KJV

SING UNTO THE LORD

I will sing unto You, Lord, a new song. You make me strong as I lift my praise to You. Praise be to God! Because of all You have done, I sing praises to You. I love to tell others how You saved me and how You help me each day. When they hear of Your marvelous ways and see You are alive and working in my life, they listen in wonder. May they, too, make You Lord of their lives.

In You I am courageous and strong. You are my joy and my strength. I will not fear. Instead, I will unceasingly sing Your praises. You are my protector. You are with me wherever I go. Thank You for Your power and might. When the challenges come, I thank You for giving me a song.

The hours tick by. Before long You will return. Then I will sing to You for eternity. Praise be to You!

PRAISE YOU FOR HEAVEN

My thoughts often turn toward Heaven, Lord. When earthly trials and worries surround me, I long to be with You. I feel homesick, as though I have some subconscious memory of having been in Heaven before. Could I have been with You there before I was placed in my mother's womb? Someday I'll have the answers.

I don't feel a part of the evil in this world and I'm certainly not attracted to what it has to offer. All the money I could earn, the treasure I can obtain, the land I may plan to buy are nothing in light of my eternal home with You. Earthly things lose their value. They wear out, rust, fade, and are sometimes stolen. The eternal treasures I store in Heaven with You can never be taken from me. So I'll invest my meager riches in You and Your work. I can't help but love You more than anything the world can give me.

Although my body will die, my soul grows closer to You with each passing day. All the trials and sufferings are minor and won't last. Thank You for the heavenly home I'll go to some day. There will be no sickness there, no pain, no tears. Only eternal life filled with joy and gladness awaits me. There I can be with You and praise You forever.

❏❏❏

Sing to the Lord a new song,
    his praise from the ends of the earth,
you who go down to the sea, and all that is in it,
    you islands, and all who live in them

Let the desert and its towns raise their voices;
    let the settlements where Kedar lives rejoice.
Let the people of Sela sing for joy;
    let them shout from the mountaintops.

                    Isaiah 42:10–11, NIV

He will wipe every tear from their eyes.
There will be no more death or
mourning or crying or pain,
for the old order of things has passed away.
Revelation 21:4, NIV

BEAUTIFUL ISLE

Somewhere, the sun is shining,
Somewhere the song-birds dwell;
Hush, then, thy sad repining,
God lives, and all is well.

Somewhere the day is long,
Somewhere the task is done;
Somewhere the heart is stronger,
Somewhere the guerdon won.

Somewhere the load is lifted,
Close by an open gate;
Somewhere the clouds are rifted,
Somewhere the angels wait.

Somewhere, Somewhere,
Beautiful Isle of Somewhere!
Land of the true, where we live anew,
Beautiful Isle of Somewhere!

Jessie B. Pounds

THANK YOU FOR OUR FOREFATHERS

For our forefathers, thank You, Lord.
For those who gave their lives,
so we could be free, thank You.

For those who dreamed new dreams,
listened to your Word,
brought revival,
won souls,
learned from Your wisdom
and passed on the lessons, thank You.

For those who sought peace,
and truth,
and justice
within our nation, thank You.

❏❏❏

Praise be to You, Father, for everlasting wisdom. A day shall come when we will be the forefathers. Grant us and our leaders an equal amount of love for You, O God, an urgency to seek Your will and ways, a dedication to build new bridges for the young. Give us each keen insight so the bridges and lessons we lay out shall withstand the tests of time.

In Jesus' name, I pray.

27

THANK YOU FOR MY COUNTRY

Lord, thank You for my country and the freedoms we have. Thank You for the huge strides we've made in science, medicine, and technology. Thank You for those who have gallantly contributed their lifework in order to help mankind.

Thank You for our Christian forefathers, for the sacrifices they made to provide us with what we have today.

When I look around, I see we have so much. Help me to be responsible in preserving the values and strengths our country began with.

In the midst of our nation's struggles, crippling hurts, and confusion, I lift our leaders (good and bad) to You in prayer for guidance and help. Grant us a godly pulsebeat, aligned with Your will and direction. Give us Christian leadership. Revive us spiritually. May we regain the standards we have so carelessly thrown away and once again become one nation under God.

Cleanse our sins and heal our land, I pray. Deliver us from drugs and violence. Help our people who love You to step forth and speak out for what is right. Help our schools, our teachers, our children to keep setting new goals, dreaming new dreams, and aiming high. Wrap Your arms around our dear country's young people and dry their tears. Lead them toward a future that is good and true. Help us to go forth as a nation, to be an example to the world, by Your love and grace.

Most of all, Lord, may I do my best to help. May

the love, kindness, and dedication begin within me.
In Jesus' name, amen.

❏❏❏

In you our fathers put their trust;
they trusted and you delivered them.
They cried to you and were saved;
in you they trusted and were not disappointed.
They will proclaim his righteousness
to a people yet unborn—for he has done it.
Psalm 22:4–5,31, NIV

If my people, who are called by my name,
will humble themselves and pray and
seek my face and turn from their wicked ways,
then will I hear from heaven and will
forgive their sin and will heal their land.
2 Chronicles 7:14, NIV

In you, O Lord, I have taken refuge;
let me never be put to shame;
deliver me in your righteousness.
Turn your ear to me, come quickly to my rescue;
be my rock of refuge, a strong fortress to save me.
Since you are my rock and my fortress,
for the sake of your name lead me and guide me.
Psalm 31:1–3, NIV

FAITH OF OUR FATHERS

Faith of our fathers! living still
In spite of dungeon, fire, and sword;
O how our hearts beat high with joy
When'er we hear that glorious word!

Faith of our fathers! we will love
Both friend and foe in all our strife;
And preach thee, too, as love knows how,
By kindly words and virtuous life;

Faith of our fathers! we will strive
To win all nations unto thee;
And through the truth that comes from God
Mankind shall then indeed be free;

Faith of our fathers, holy faith!
We will be true to thee till death!

Frederick William Faber

Love Comes from You

Lord, You often remind us to love and care for our families first. At times we American families are so busy being thoughtful to those outside our homes that we forget the ones who are most important. Our families deserve our best manners, our best attention, and our first love, second to God.

Instead, at times we forget our thoughtful and kind ways and mistreat each other. Perhaps we think our families will put up with our actions, because they love us "just the way we are." Must we play mind games or belittle and manipulate the ones we love? Must we say hurtful things to get our way or to get our points across? How sad. This must grieve You terribly, Lord. It is so wrong and so destructive. Forgive us for such sinful actions.

Help us treat our spouses, children, and other loved ones with kindness, to cherish and care for them. Help us to avoid careless words that may injure for a lifetime. May we treasure these dear ones and share their joys and concerns and dreams. May our foremost time and effort be with the ones we love the most. Let us show them the love we talk about so freely, so our families will grow strong and secure in You.

Lord, we know we cannot have strong family units without following Your teachings. You know our hearts. Let our lives please You.

SERVICE

Lord of all pots and pans and things
since I've no time to be
A saint by doing lovely things,
or watching late with Thee,
Or dreaming in the dawnlight,
or storming heaven's gates,
Make me a saint by getting meals,
and washing up the plates.

Although I must have Martha's hand,
I have a Mary's mind;
And when I black the boots and shoes,
Thy sandals, Lord, I find,
I think of how they trod the earth,
each time I scrub the floor;
Accept this meditation, Lord,
I haven't time for more.

Warm all the kitchen with Thy love,
and light it with Thy peace,
Forgive me all my worrying,
and make all grumbling cease.
Thou who didst love to give me food,
in room or by sea,
Accept this service that I do—
I do it unto Thee.

Author Unknown

MY OWN PRIVATE ALTAR

Lord, family strife is crushing in again. I've tried making peace between family members before but I've found myself caught in the middle. Now, though, I've discovered my own private altar.

Each time when the hurt feelings fly, I retreat to that altar and raise our needs to You. A peace settles on our home. You intervene where I can't and You bring love back where it belongs.

Once again I retreat from the clamor and bickering. I silently slip through the door. I close and lock it. On my knees by my altar, I lift my heart in praise, urgent petition, and love. Ah, yes! I can already hear the peace, and I sense Your work has begun.

Thank You, Lord, for my own private altar. My knees press on hard tile with one little rug. The air is filled with disinfectant. My elbows rest on smooth porcelain. Though my prayer room is my bathroom, my altar my bathtub, at this moment it is my holy of holies.

My heart rejoices in You. I return to my duties until the next time I come here to meet with You.

❏❏❏

But when you pray, do not be like the hypocrites, for they love to pray standing in the synagogues and on the street corners to be seen by men. I tell you the truth, they have received their reward in full. But when you pray, go into your room, close the door and pray to your Father, who is unseen. Then your Father who sees what is done in secret, will reward you.

Matthew 6:5–6, NIV

SOMEONE PRAYED FOR ME

Today was one of those days, Lord, where everything seemed to go wrong. There were many anxious moments. All of a sudden I felt calm. You were able to give me a perspective that helped me through. Was someone praying for me?

THREE DAYS LATER:

A note arrived from a friend. It told how she had thought of me and prayed at a certain time. When I recalled the day and time, I remembered my crisis. Thank You, Lord, for laying my burdens on the heart of a dear friend, when I most needed her prayers.

❑❑❑

In the same way, the Spirit helps us in our weakness. We do not know what we ought to pray, but the Spirit himself intercedes for us with groans that words cannot express. And he who searches our hearts knows the mind of the Spirit, because the Spirit intercedes for the saints in accordance with God's will.

Romans 8:26–27, NIV

THANK YOU FOR YOUR NUDGE

Another chaotic day. My mind is kicked into accelerated speed. Responsibilities—schedules—deadlines. Accomplishments well-done in a normal workday world. Then I feel Your nudge. I recognize Your voice. I've felt that nudge so many times before. Over and over you prod me, like a child tugging at his mother's sleeve to gain my attention.

You finally get me to listen. Someone comes to mind. I realize the need to pray. Now! I may not even know why. The world stops around me. I offer silent prayer. With powerful wings Your Holy Spirit swiftly wafts my petition for the one in need to almighty God.

You bring the prayer need to mind repeatedly throughout the day. I keep praying.

Later, when I hear the story of the one I prayed for, I marvel at Your timing and wisdom.

Thank You, Lord, for Your nudge.

❑❑❑

Shew me thy ways,
O Lord; teach me thy paths.
Lead me in thy truth, and teach me:
for thou art the God of my salvation;
on thee do I wait all the day.
Psalm 25:4–6, KJV

FLIP SIDE OF NEGATIVE

There are times in this world I see and hear so much of the negative, Father, that I'm tempted to get caught up in it. Then I think of You. I can't change others, only myself.

Thank You for helping me see the good in people, the best in difficult situations. Let me sense the fresh smell of drizzling cleansing rain, the quiet times during recovering illness. Thank You for teaching me to recall the good events in life and help me not to dwell on the bad ones.

Thank You for helping me see the good even in myself. I will build on that rather than put myself down.

I lift my praise to You in all situations and look for Your goodness and love.

Rejoice in the Lord always, I will say it again: Rejoice! Let your gentleness be evident to all. The Lord is near. Do not be anxious about anything, but in everything, by prayer and petition, with thanksgiving, present your requests to God. And the peace of God, which transcends all understanding, will guard your hearts and minds in Christ Jesus.

Finally, brothers, whatever is true, whatever is noble, whatever is right, whatever is pure, whatever is lovely, whatever is admirable—if anything is excellent or praiseworthy—think about such things.

Philippians 4:4–8, NIV

THANK YOU FOR YOUR WORD

Thank You for my Bible, Your Word. How dear it is to me. Each day I draw nourishment and direction from it. How rich its words are! How healing and comforting Your promises, in times of weariness and stress. Your Word never fails me. It is like a map for me to find my way. I open it and marvel at all its wisdom. Thank You for providing these Scriptures so I can find direction in my life.

How perceptive are Your teachings. What blessings I receive from reading its words. You are so wonderful to give me the secrets to having a joy-filled life.

Still there are mysteries to unfold as I read its

fathomless insights. How can I ever fully understand all of the lessons? Will I ever be able to completely know the mind of God? You are too great for me to do so.

How could I possibly have a pure heart without Your Scriptures to remind and guide each day? I would have no direction or hope.

I seek You with all my being so I might not stray. I memorize and hide Your words in my heart. When temptation and testing come, I can draw on what I have learned as Your Son Jesus did when He was tempted.

Praise You, dear Lord. Teach me Your countless lessons. I will repeat them on my lips and hide them in my heart as You have shown me. I will rejoice in all I learn. I will meditate on Your Word and praise You through my nights and days.

❏❏❏

I have hidden your word in my heart
    that I might not sin against you.
Praise be to you, O Lord;
    teach me your decrees.
With my lips I will recount
    all the laws that come from your mouth.
I rejoice in following your statutes
    as one rejoices in great riches.
I meditate on your precepts
    and consider your ways.
I delight in your decrees;
    I will not neglect your word.

Psalm 119:11–16, NIV

PRAISING YOU AT DAWN

I wake in the hush of night with dawn lacing together shadows and shimmers, silhouetted by a silvery moon. I slip outside and listen to the silence. Might I hear Your voice? A cool rush of wind passes through. I see a small wild animal dart from bush to bush, unaware of my presence. I didn't realize such animals were so near. The wind whispers quietly as if to say, "Be still and know God is also near."

A rooster crows from afar, greeting dawn before I even see it. A robin signals to her family from a nearby tree. In wisdom You so magnificently made it all.

A pale blue glow creeps across the sky, first caressing the trees, then kissing the flowers with tiny drops of dew. "Savor this moment," I feel You say. "Carry the strength I give into your busy, strenuous day. My Spirit goes with you. Take time today to bless others."

Ah, yes, Lord, I will.

❏❏❏

Another morning, the persistent chirp of a mother robin outside our bedroom window awakened me. I glanced at the clock. 4:30 A.M. How can birds be awake so early? I wondered.

I found myself alert, as though a quiet voice were beckoning me to our backyard patio. I slipped on my robe, tiptoed to the kitchen, and quietly prepared a cup of hot tea. The crisp, gently breeze caressed my cheeks when I pushed back the sliding glass door. I settled into my favorite patio chair—just me, my cup of tea, and best of all, my Lord.

"Be still and know that I am God," I felt Him whisper on the wind.

I knew I would soon be challenged with endless responsibilities in the next few days. I had already asked for His help. In the solitude of a backyard heavenly chapel, the Lord and I shared secrets, concerns, and direction for an hour and a half. I thought I would be tired. Instead, I felt exhilarated by His Spirit.

I frequently return to my favorite spot while the whole world sleeps. There I regain the strength and guidance He always has to give.

> Give ear to my words, O Lord,
> consider my meditation. . .
> My voice shalt thou hear in the morning, O Lord;
> in the morning will I direct my prayer unto thee,
> and will look up.
> Psalm 5:1, 3, KJV

THANK YOU FOR YOUR WONDROUS WORKS

Thank You, Lord, for Your wondrous works and all the things You do for me. I praise You with my whole heart and soul. So many times You shower Your mercy on me and forgive my sins. You reach down and heal my tired body. Your love, mercy, and patience go beyond measure. You help me in my depths of despair and actually pump new life and enthusiasm into me.

I marvel at how You roll out the star-filled sky like a scroll. The oceans look as though You have scooped them out with Your mighty hand. Even the winds and waves are in Your control. You care about the wild birds and animals. How grateful I am that You also care for me.

You are my King of Kings. How I love You, Lord. I will praise You and strive to be a blessing to You forever.

Bless the Lord, O my soul.
O Lord my God, thou art very great;
thou are clothed with honour and majesty.
Who coverest thyself with light as with a garment:
who stretchest out the heavens like a curtain:
Who layeth the beams of his chambers in the waters:
who maketh the clouds his chariot:
who walketh upon the wings of the wind.

Man goeth forth unto his work and
to his labour until evening.
O Lord, how manifold are thy works!
In wisdom hast thou made them all:
the earth is full of thy riches.

I will sing unto the Lord as long as I live:
I will sing praise to my God while I have my being.
My meditation of him shall be sweet:
I will be glad in the Lord.
Psalm 104:1–3; 23–24; 33–34, KJV

THANK YOU FOR MAKING ME ME

Father, my nose is crooked, my hair's too straight, my curves are bulges and definitely in wrong places! I'm not too smart, and I'm always sticking my foot in my mouth. This is what I think of me when my thoughts are not on You.

You know me so well. You see my every thought, no matter how trivial. All my ways are discerned by You. You hear the words I say before they roll off my tongue. (Help me to bite some before they leave my mouth.) You surround me with Your love and have Your hand on me at all times.

How can You have such magnificent knowledge, too marvelous for me to attain? You are with me everywhere, any time. You are with me in the night time and the beginning of a brand new day. I even awake to Your presence.

You created my innermost being and molded me in my mother's womb. You knew the color of my hair and eyes and the shape of my nose before I was ever born, so now I thank You for them. How can I question my funny looks and ways? I give You praise, instead, that You created such a miracle in me and started my heart beating. How can I comprehend Your mighty works?

I must be precious to You, for You love me as I am. This is all so awesome to me. Search my heart, dear Lord. Cleanse me from evil and change me as You wish. See my thoughts. Understand my concerns and set my mind at ease.

I'm glad I'm me and I'm thankful that You made me. I want to be a blessing for You—just the way I am.

HIS ANSWER

My child, the delight of My heart, you are a gift to Me. Before I formed you in your mother's womb, I already knew you well. I knew your talents and abilities that would someday bless Me and others. You are beautiful in My sight. I love you just the way you are. I made a place in this world especially for you. I've prepared a future for you to serve Me.

You are a flower in life's garden, My special one. Your color and sweet fragrance is lovely and treasured.

At times you feel afraid, unsure of what you do. Remember, I am with you, helping, guiding all the way as you serve Me. Now, My child, I reach out My hands and touch yours, I touch your feet, your mouth, your mind. Receive then My power and serve Me.

Read Psalm 139:1–6; 13–14.

I'M PROUD OF MY ACCOMPLISHMENTS

Father, I'm proud of my accomplishments. Not the kind of pride that brags, but the kind that makes me feel pleased and warm inside. I've worked hard on this project, yet I couldn't have done it without You. Thank You, Father, for Your guidance and help.

Thank You for teaching me to set realistic goals for myself. Thank You for challenging me to do my best. Thank You for showing me how to love You first, then to love myself, as well as others.

If my accomplishments should go unrecognized, no matter. I feel good about them. Best of all, I know You are proud of me and that You love me.

❏❏❏

I am the vine, ye are the branches:
He that abideth in me, and I in him,
the same bringeth forth much fruit:
for without me ye can do nothing.
John 15:5, KJV

I can do all things through Christ
which strengtheneth me.
Philippians 4:13, KJV

YOU SAID I COULD DO IT

Some said I couldn't do it.
Some shook their heads in doubt.
Some rolled their eyes and sighed.
"You can never work it out."

You said I could do it:
The task You gave to me.
I worked from dawn through dusk,
With help that came from Thee.

And now that it's complete,
New goals You place ahead.
I'm glad I showed You honor,
And heard Your voice instead.

PART 2

REPENTANCE

O HAPPY DAY, THAT FIXED MY CHOICE

O happy day, that fixed my choice
    On Thee, my Saviour and my God!
Well may this glowing heart rejoice,
    And tell its raptures all abroad.

'Tis done; the great transaction's done!
    I am my Lord's, and He is mine;
He drew me, and I followed on,
    Charmed to confess the voice divine.

Philip Doddridge

I will greatly rejoice in the Lord, for my soul shall be joyful in my God; for he hath clothed me with the garments of salvation, he hath covered me with the robe of righteousness, as a bridegroom decketh himself with ornaments, and as a bride adorneth herself with her jewels.

Isaiah 61:10, KJV

GOSSIP

I opened my mouth before I thought. Forgive me, Lord. How could I have talked so behind someone's back? I can never retrieve careless words.

Give me strength to ask for forgiveness, to try to make things right. Go before me, dear Lord, and help me make amends.

I am beginning to realize gossip cuts to the core. Wise words soothe and heal. Teach me, Lord, to use words of wisdom, and in the future let me remember the hard lesson from this experience. Guard my tongue and seal my lips. The Bible shows me that careless words can break bones.

May I not get caught in the snares of others who are gossiping. Help me to build up life's cornerstones in people, rather than chiseling and breaking them down.

Fill my thoughts with things that are good and right. Let everything I do and say be pleasing to You.

Now, I focus my eyes on You, dear Lord. I take refuge in Your strength and comfort in Your wisdom.

GOSSIP

When careless words are spoken.
To be retrieved no more,
Lay each one at Christ's altar,
Then go and sin no more.

Read 1 Timothy 5:13; James 3:13–18.

❑❑❑

Peacemakers who sow in peace
raise a harvest of righteousness.
James 3:18, NIV

THE ARGUMENT

Lord, I did it again. I fell into another argument and spoke unkindly. Why was I so thoughtless? My heart feels heavy; I find myself replaying the disagreement all day. Can I be wrong although I know I'm "right"?

Is my attitude pure, unconditional love?

Please, calm my emotions. Help us to talk, to show respect, and to listen rather than argue.

When I must disagree, help me express my feelings with love, doing my best to keep this person's dignity intact. Show me how to separate the essential from the trivial, and to know where I should give in. In spite of our differences, I must remain accepting of the one I love.

Has it been seventy times seven that I have forgiven? Help me show gentleness and forgiveness as You do. Let me be willing not to hold a grudge. Teach me to go beyond myself with thoughtfulness and kindness during this time, remembering that perfect love casts out fear.

Surround me and my loved one with Your presence and keep us nestled in Your pure, sweet love.

Linda sputtered at her husband Don and stormed out, angry enough to walk five miles. After a few blocks her pace lessened. Her racing mind settled. She clutched her sweater with folded arms. Was she cold from the evening air or from chilling words she had spoken? Did it really matter who was right or wrong? Linda thought of how defensive she'd become from her husband's comment. Could it be because there was some truth to what he'd said? She rounded another neighborhood block, afraid to apologize. What if he wouldn't listen? Must she state her view again?

Linda remembered the Bible verse: "Perfect love drives out fear" 1 John 4:18, NIV. Her conscience gently chided, "There is no need for excuses, just love."

Her pace quickened and Linda headed for home. When she approached their front yard, she could see the warm glow of living room lights. She quietly opened the door and paused, welcomed by Don's open arms. "I'm sorry," she cried.

"So am I."

"How could I have been so thoughtless?"

"We'll work it out."

"I'll try to understand."

The chill left. Love's warmth returned.

There is no fear in love.
But perfect love drives out fear,
because fear has to do with punishment.
The one who fears
is not made perfect in love.
We love because he first loved us.
1 John 4:18–19, NIV

PART 3

FORGIVENESS

I MET THE MASTER FACE TO FACE

I had walked life's path with an easy tread
Had followed where comfort and pleasure led;
And then one day in a quiet place
I met the Master, face to face.

With station and rank and wealth for a goal
Much thought for the body, but none for the soul;
I had thought to win in life's mad race,
When I met the Master, face to face.

I had built my castles and reared them high,
Till their towers pierced the blue of the sky,
I had vowed to rule with an iron mace,
When I met the Master, face to face.

I met Him and knew Him, and blushed to see
That His eyes full of sorrow were turned on me;
And I faltered, and fell at His feet that day,
While all my castles melted away.

Melted and vanished, and in their place
I saw nothing else but my Master's face;
And I cried aloud: "Oh, make me meet
To follow the path of Thy wounded feet."

And now my thoughts are for souls of men,
I've lost my life, to find it again.
E'er since that day in a quiet place
I met the Master, face to face.

Author Unknown

HELP ME FORGIVE

I've been hurt again, Lord. Not only me, but the ones I love. I'm angry at the cruelty. I know there is no remorse. If the ones who hurt me had it to do again, they'd do the same things. I want to lash out. I want to get even. I know this isn't how You want me to react. My hatred and anger can harm many people, myself, and my relationship with You and others, Lord. I can't seem to forgive or change my attitudes. Please help me. I pray that You will take away my pain and wrong attitudes.

I've done all I can to work things out with no success. Now I seek Your direction and will. I know You command me to love and pray for others, even my enemies. Although their actions are wrong, help me to respond in the right way. Remind me not to rejoice when they meet trouble, but to pray continually for them. Guard my tongue against speaking unkind words. Help me to have a pure heart and leave the rest in Your hands.

Because I submit to You, I sense Your help and peace in this situation. I'm learning how much love You must have to forgive me.

No matter how hard she tried, Susan couldn't forgive her daughter Alyssa and her friends for what they had done during their rebellious teenage years. Now an adult, something was keeping Alyssa from living a victorious Christian life. What could it be? Susan prayed for her often but couldn't identify the problem.

The Lord spoke to Susan's heart. He showed her that until she could forgive, she too was in sin. He helped her realize the hurt and anger she felt were linked together and that she had to let go of both in order to truly forgive. Susan asked God to help her forgive and let go of the painful memories.

The next time Alyssa came to visit, Susan's heart was free from fear, hurt, and bitterness. She and Alyssa took a long walk on a hiking trail shortly before the daughter was to return to her own home. As they walked and visited, Alyssa noticed something different about her mother and asked what it was. The mother told Alyssa how God had helped her change. She assured her daughter of the pride and of the unconditional love she felt for Alyssa. A bond of joy and freedom they hadn't experienced for years returned to mother and daughter. No excuses for shortcomings were offered by either—just "sorries" and forgiveness.

Soon after, Alyssa's love for the Lord matured. Susan felt thankful she was finally able to forgive, love, and step out of God's way, so He could work.

❑❑❑

". . . Forgive and you will be forgiven."
Luke 6:37, NIV

THANK YOU FOR YOUR FORGIVENESS

Father, my heart cries out with sorrow and regret for the sin I've committed. How can I possibly forgive myself for such a deed? I know I've hurt You, because You love me so. I try and try to do what is right I but just mess up time after time. Please forgive me and help me to forgive myself.

In Jesus' name.

THE ANSWER

My dear child, what other times?
I've washed all that away with my blood.
Forgive as I forgive you.
Love, Jesus

JESUS: WHAT A FRIEND FOR SINNERS

Jesus! what a friend for sinners!
Jesus! lover of my soul;
Friends may fail me, foes assail me,
He, my Savior, makes me whole.

Jesus! what a help in sorrow!
While the billows o'er me roll,
Even when my heart is breaking,
He, my comfort, helps my soul.

J. Wilbur Chapman

PART 4

DEDICATION

I WOULD BE TRUE

I would be true, for there are those who trust me;
I would be pure, for there are those who care,
I would be strong, for there is much to suffer;
I would be brave, for there is much to dare.

I would be friend of all—the foe, the friendless,
I would be giving, and forget the gift.
I would be humble, for I know my weakness;
I would look up, and laugh, and love, and lift.

I would be prayerful, through each busy moment,
I would be constantly in touch with God.
I would be tuned to hear His slightest whisper;
I would have faith to keep the path Christ trod.

Howard Al Walter

HIS BEST

God has His best things for the few
Who dare to stand the test,
God has His second choice for those
Who will not take His best.
And others make the highest choice,
But when by trials pressed,
They shrink, they yield, they shun the Cross,
And so they lose His best.

I want in this short life of mine
As much as can be pressed
Of service true for God and man—
Help me to be Thy best.
I want among the victor-throng
To have my name confessed,
And hear the Master say at last—
"Well done! you did your best."

Author Unknown

THE TEACHER'S PRAYER

Father, I long to instill important lessons in my students' minds that will last a lifetime. Some days I am not at my best. Forgive me when I fail.

You chose me to teach children. You placed in my care excellent students looking for challenges and troubled students looking for ways out of their problems. Help me to never let them down.

Help me remember to praise and recognize every child's efforts and accomplishments. Make my activities purposeful with realistic goals. Teach me to be firm but loving, direct but tactful. Help me mold lives so they may become wise.

When the so-called impossible child challenges me, help me to be consistent, hearing each need and expecting only the best of which each is capable. When I've done all I can and still can't get through to a child, let me hold him or her up in prayer, trusting You to accomplish things I can't.

Help me remember I'm also a child, Your child. Dear Father, help me never forget the way You treat me.

Let everything I do and say be pleasing to You and beneficial to the kids I teach. Go before and behind me doing Your good and acceptable will.

Thank You, Father, for Your guidance.

THE SECRET

Stacy sighed and unlocked her classroom door. Teaching had become a task instead of a joy. What had happened to her enthusiasm and creativity? "Should I leave teaching?" she murmured. "God, please help me."

Stacy dropped her bag by the desk and tackled a science project. She could hear her friend Geraldine humming next door, as usual.

Geraldine's been in the district forever, *Stacy pondered.* How does she always stay on top?

Just then, her friend popped into the room with a sunshiny smile. "Hi, Stacy. How are you doing?"

Stacy leaned back and tapped her pencil against the science text. "I'm burning out. I feel it and I think the kids can, too. It's so much harder than it used to be." She threw her arms toward her classroom desks. Her voice croaked with frustration. "There's so many more discipline problems and the struggles these kids face break my heart. I seem to be getting nowhere. How do you stay so positive?" Stacy's voice lowered to a whisper. "What's your secret?"

Geraldine pulled up a chair and brushed a wisp of graying hair from her eyes. "There's no secret, Stacy. I have my tough days, too. Sometimes I'm overwhelmed. That's when I really pray for help."

She laughed. "One time I told the Lord I felt totally alone in trying to solve all these kids' problems. That's when He spoke to my heart and asked if I thought He would leave the world to someone like me to run—or could He do it for me?

"Now, no matter how busy I am, I pray for each student first thing everyday. That's my source of strength and joy."

Before long Stacy changed her perspective. She saw many prayers answered and with God's help regained her joy and enthusiasm.

THE TEACHER'S PRAYER

Let me love a child more dearly every day.
Let me help the child who struggles find his way.
Let me stop to see his needs and gently pray.

Then may this day be right,
Within Your guiding light,
I humbly pray.

❏❏❏

May the words of my mouth and
the meditation of my heart,
be pleasing in your sight,
O Lord, my Rock and my Redeemer.
Psalm 19:14, NIV

BALANCING THE BUDGET

Dear Father, how can I pay these bills? Sometimes I don't even know where food money will come from. I'm working as hard as possible, but on paper I can't meet the budget.

I give it to You, dear Lord. I place myself and these bills in Your hands and ask for Your direction. Show me how I can help others even while I hurt financially. Help me share a portion of my earning with You for Your glory. Remind me to give You first place in my pocket book!

Teach me to be prudent in my spending, wise in my financial decisions, and responsible in attempting to pay my obligations.

Enable me to trust You to provide for my needs so I won't worry about food or drink, money or clothes. You already know my needs. I thank You for providing.

Let me not be anxious about tomorrow. I know You will take care of that, too. I will take each day as it comes and commit it to You.

I will trust You, Lord, and not lean on my own understanding of these situations. Instead, with all my might, I will recognize Your will to direct my paths.

God owns our money,
>   our homes.
God owns the land our homes stand on,
>   our cars.
God owns our clothes,
>   all our treasures.

God wants us to help others,
>   our churches.
God wants us to be trustworthy,
>   responsible.
God wants us to take care of what we have,
>   to submit all and trust in Him.

❑❑❑

Therefore I tell you, do not worry about your life,
>   what you will eat or drink;
>   or about your body, what you will wear. . . .
>   Look at the birds of the air . . .
>   your heavenly Father feeds them.
>   Are you not more valuable than they?. . .
But seek first his kingdom and his righteousness,
and all these things will be given to you as well.
>   Matthew 5:25–26, 33, NIV

GROWING OLDER

Lord, that big zero in my age just rounded the corner. My friends tease me about being over the hill. They say the best of life is gone. When I hear this, I laugh.

I wonder what You have in store for me this next year? How can You use me during this phase of my life? I have no fear of growing older. Life is out there to enjoy. Thank You for giving me one more year to do so.

I will not be poured into an ancient mold. I may be growing older, but I refuse to act old. Old age is an attitude. I'm determined to live life abundantly through Your joy and strength.

I see the trees with their scars and burls. Reflecting Your glorious sunset, their branches reach heavenward and praise You, O God. They have survived many of life's storms, just like me. In the still of evening I can hear their rustling boughs whisper a night wind's song, thanking You for life.

I'm not ashamed of pain-filled fingers gnarled from arthritis. They show the work I have done for others. I see the wrinkles collecting on my face. Character lines, I call them. I especially like the ones put there from years of smiles. No matter my health, I can always find ways to serve You, such as letters to the lonely. Best of all, I can hold others up in faithful prayer.

I thank You, Lord, for life and that You offer it to me in an abundance of spirit and joy. Even when I reach my sunset years, I lift my praise to You. May I reflect Your Holy Spirit all the days of my life.

❑❑❑

Strength and honour are her clothing; and she shall rejoice in time to come. She openeth her mouth with wisdom; and in her tongue is the law of kindness. . . . Favour is deceitful, and beauty is vain: but a woman that feareth the Lord, she shall be praised.

Proverbs 31:25–26; 30, KJV

Jaw set, Orlan bent his head in prayer. His silvery hair reflected the church sanctuary lights. The ninety-year-old man's eyes shut tightly as he went to war again. Like many other times, Orlan engaged in a spiritual battle through prayer. The need? No matter. Yet one of many answered victoriously.

Orlan's wife, Jessie, sat near him. She squeezed his hand and joined him in prayer. The Holy Spirit surrounded them—perhaps angels hovered, rejoicing, protecting.

Orlan and Jessie have served the Lord most of their lives. They have built churches, taught Sunday school classes, prayed without ceasing, and won souls for Him. Now they move much slower from arthritis, poor eyesight, and dulled hearing. But they keep going and doing for the Lord!

When asked about retirement, they shake their heads and say, "There's too much work to be done." Besides prayer, Orlan is always willing to help wherever possible. Jessie writes cards and notes of cheer.

Both willingly lend a hand even when not feeling well.

We must keep using the valuable older people in our churches. They are our cornerstones, our legacies.

They have so much wisdom and experience to offer. Some have given their entire lives for Christ and the church. If they are put on a shelf, their joy in life is snuffed out. God certainly isn't finished with them yet!

As I grow older, I pray I will be allowed to keep a vision, compassion, and dedication, so I can serve God with all my strength and being.

Thank you, Orlan, Jessie, and other older folks for your service and prayers. Keep on keeping on.

❑❑❑

Listen, my son, to your father's instruction
and do not forsake your mother's teaching.
They will be a garland to grace your head
and a chain to adorn your neck.
Proverbs 1:8–9, NIV

❑❑❑

I DEDICATE MY HEART TO YOU

Father, I give You my heart, my soul, my life. I dedicate my whole being to You. I give You my failures and my successes, my fears and my aspirations.

Search my heart. Let my thoughts and motives be pure. You know me through and through. Remove the unclean ways in me that I might be pleasing to You.

Fill me with Your spirit, I pray; enable me to do the tasks set before me. Lead me into Your everlasting way.

Wherever I go, whatever the challenge, I pray that You will be there, guiding me completely. From my rising in the morn to my resting at night, O Lord, be near, surrounding me continually with Your love.

I look forward with joyful anticipation to what You have planned for me. Thank You for becoming Lord of my life.

❑❑❑

Search me, O God, and know my heart;
test me and know my anxious thoughts.
See if there is any offensive way in me,
and lead me in the way everlasting.
Psalm 139:23–24, NIV

One of the most difficult things about dedicating our all to God is relinquishing control. We don't know what He has in store for us. We are fearful it may be too difficult or uncomfortable. Often we worry that we won't be able to measure up.

We must remember God knows our future, He has our concerns and best interests at heart. Along the way we may not understand the reasoning of His direction for us. As we continue walking by faith in the paths He blazes, we'll learn His answers.

Take each step, obey, and fear not. One day, one moment at a time is all He asks. When troubles come, look to Him, plant your feet on His path, and dig in your toes. Don't waver! He'll show the best way. He has already walked the path.

PART 5

GRIEF

IN THE HOUR OF TRIAL

In the hour of trial,
Jesus, plead for me,
Lest by base denial
I depart from Thee.
When Thou seest me waver,
With a look recall,
Nor for fear or favor
Suffer me to fall.

Should Thy mercy send me
Sorrow, toil and woe,
Or should pain attend me
On my path below.
Grant that I may never
Fail Thy hand to see;
Grant that I may ever
Cast my care on Thee.
Amen

James Montgomery

MY LOVED ONE HAS GONE

Dear Lord, I miss my loved one so. Since this dear one has died, there's a huge gap in my life. Will it ever be filled? In all this, I thank You for friends and family who show they care. Grant me energy to reach out to them in return and to accept and give love. Perhaps it will help fill some of the emptiness.

Comfort and help me find my way through all of this. Let me recall and cherish the good times, to let the bad memories go.

How can I bear my loss? I long for the one who was so full of life and beauty, like the roses outside my window. My roses will fade from winter's chill, and so, too, have I seen my loved one fade. I gaze at my lovely garden with its splendid array of color. I'm reminded that my dear one who loved You will blossom in full glory for You in Heaven.

I take comfort in Your presence and cling to the assurance that You, the Rose of Sharon, will always abide with me.

Think of stepping on shore and finding it Heaven!
　　Of taking hold of a hand and finding it God's,
Of breathing new air, and finding it celestial air,
　　Of feeling invigorated, and finding it immortality,
Of passing from storm and tempest to an unbroken
　　calm,
　　Of waking up, and finding it Home!

Anonymous

□□□

The grass withereth, the flower fadeth: but the word
of our God shall stand forever.   Isaiah 40:8, KJV

How can a void be filled and pain eased from losing a
loved one or friend? Did that one walk with the Lord?
Or are we left to wonder? Either way, grief remains—
deep, sharp with no solace in sight.

On the day of the funeral it often rains. If not out-
wardly, in our hearts. How appropriate. It matches the
tears we shed.

Yet, as a glimmer of sunlight cuts through our rain,
we see again God's everlasting promise arrayed in glorious color. Each shade reminds us of His many promises:

Red, for His love (John 3:16).
Orange, His warm healing and comfort
    (Matthew 5:4).
Yellow, the sun that will shine again
    (Jeremiah 31:13).
Green, His help for us to grow (1 Peter 2:2).
Blue, His unending faithfulness (Psalm 56:3–4).
Indigo, we are children of the King (Luke 20:36).
Violet, a new song to return in His time
    (Song of Solomon 2:12).

As we focus on His love and Word, in time He
will fill our void and loneliness and heal our pain.

DEPRESSION

My nights are sleepless again, dear Lord. Shadows creep around my room. I toss and turn in anguish. When I finally do sleep, I bolt up in bed, frightened that something or someone is after me.

I realize I need Your help more than ever. Life is too tough for me to handle. Lead me to people who can help. Open my mind to ways for me to overcome this terrible depression.

At times I am so distraught I can't even pray. Yet Your Holy Spirit knows my heart. I know You are lifting my needs to my Heavenly Father in words that can never be expressed by any human. I take comfort in that.

Let me give my burdens all to You, my Lord. I must let You carry them for me. Most of all, help me be willing not to take them back.

I know You watch over me and will help me through this. I put my trust in You. I won't depend on my own understanding. I purpose to acknowledge You in every way and be alert to Your direction. Let me not worry. Help me do my best to solve each problem as it comes along and pray about everything, large and small. Here are my anxieties and my problems. I thank You for Your answers, given according to Your will. You know my needs before I ask.

In doing this, I pray that You grant me peace of heart beyond my comprehension. (Peace is not the absence of problems but a new perspective from You for my life.) Guard my mind and soul against all that isn't honorable to You or best for my well-being.

Finally, dear Lord, enable me to fix my thoughts on You and things that are positive, true and worthy of praise. No matter what kind of circumstances I am in, let me be content in Your leading. Whether I am well-fed or hungry, in plenty or want, healthy or ill, I know You will guide me through by Your strength.

Thank You, Lord, for Your love and peace. Thank You that You will meet my needs.

I love You, in Jesus' name.

AND CAN IT BE

Long my imprisoned spirit lay,
    Fast bound in sin and nature's night;
Thine eye diffused a quickening ray,
    I woke, the dungeon flamed with light:
My chains fell off, my heart was free,
    I rose, went forth, and followed Thee.

Charles Wesley

Peace I leave with you . . .
I do not give to you as the world gives.
Do not let your hearts be troubled
and do not be afraid.
John 14:27, NIV

LORD, TAKE ME HOME

At times like this, Lord, I can hardly stand all the hurts, tragedies, and sin in this world. I'm forced to brush shoulders with it every day.

It grieves me when loved ones and friends fall away from you, marriages dissolve, and disaster strikes, over and over. What bothers me most is when I see little children suffer from abuse, illness, and neglect. Lord, please take me Home, I'm tired of being here. I feel ashamed to pray this way. But, oh, the pain. Thank You for loving me in my weakest moments.

I read in Your Word when You said, "Not My will, but Thine be done." If you need to keep me here, so be it, dear Lord, although I long to be with You. As long as You have a purpose for me, I will serve You with all my heart. Grant me comfort and strength, I pray. And, Father, when you're finished with me here, I'm ready to come home to You.

❑❑❑

TAKE ME HOME

What is this tugging at my heart?
'Tis like a homing dove.
How can I long for a place unseen.
And feel His endless love?

Homesick and worn, I strive each day,
A broken soul to love.
But my broken heart aches to join,
My Savior up above.

How long must I fight the battles,
On tearstained fields for Thee?
"Until your task is finished here,"
He firmly says to me.

"I've covered your scars with my blood.
I've washed your hands and feet.
I've taken the sins of your soul.
To the mercy seat."

What love I feel in His voice,
His hands outstretched to me.
I'll serve until that moment,
His loving face I see.

MY CHILD IS NOT WHOLE

Dear Lord, help my child who isn't whole. Why does my little one have to be this way? Why does such a precious child have these deficiencies? Sometimes I blame myself. If I had done this or that, would it have made a difference? My heart aches, longing for things to be better. I wish I could understand.

I love my child so much. Even though this dear one is disabled, to me I have the most wonderful little one in the world. I thank You for giving me such a sweet gift. Could my child be an angel in disguise?

Grant me patience daily, yet give me determination and consistency. Give me wisdom as I expect my child to do the best that abilities provide, yet let me be realistic in my expectations. Remind me to praise and accent the little accomplishments; help me build self-esteem. Let me cherish each day for the good times. Grant me strength when I am weak and weary, a calm spirit when I am frustrated.

Use this child, I pray, to be a blessing for You and those nearby. Let me learn from my experiences, and let me be of help to others with children who also are not whole.

Thank You, Lord, for giving me my child. Remind me that in Your eyes this little one is whole.

Jesus said,
"Let the little children come to me,
and do not hinder them,
for the kingdom of heaven
belongs to such as these."
Matthew 19:14, NIV

THE BLIND CHILD

I know what Mother's face is like,
Although I cannot see;
It's like the music of a bell
It's like the roses I can smell.
Yes, these it's like to me.
I know what Father's face is like
I'm sure I know it all;
It's like his whistle on the air;
It's like his arms which take such care,
And never let me fall.

And I can tell what God is like,
The God whom no one sees.
He's everything my parents seem;
He's fairer than my fondest dream,
Still greater than all these.

Anonymous

Part 6
Healing

How Sweet the Name of Jesus Sounds

How sweet the name of Jesus sounds
In a believer's ear!
It soothes his sorrows, heals his wounds,
And drives away his fear.

It makes the wounded spirit whole,
And calms the troubled breast;
'Tis manna to the hungry soul,
And to the weary, rest.

Jesus, my Shepherd, Guardian, Friend,
My Prophet, Priest, and King,
My Lord, my Life, my Way, my End,
Accept the praise I bring.
Amen.

John Newton

Give ear, O Lord, unto my prayer;
and attend to the voice of my supplications.
In the day of my trouble I will call upon thee;
for thou wilt answer me.

Teach me thy way, O Lord;
I will walk in thy truth:
unite my heart to fear thy name.

O turn unto me, and have mercy upon me;
give thy strength unto thy servant. . . .

I will praise thee, O Lord my God,
with all my heart:
and I will glorify thy name for evermore.
Psalm 86:6–7, 11, 16, 12, KJV

PICK UP THE BROKEN PIECES

Father, I am broken. I seem to be filled with absolute emptiness. I have nothing to offer You but pieces of my life. Pick them up, I pray, and use them. Help me submit, while You arrange these pieces in a new way. I understand Your way is best. You are the Master Craftsman and know my very being. Thank You for the miracle You create from my shattered life. Thank You for how You are making me into a beautiful new vessel to be used for You.

In Jesus' name, I pray.

PIECES REPAIRED

Melissa lay shattered, like a priceless, broken vase. Irreparable, it seemed. Too much sadness had come her way. Doctors, psychiatrists, friends, and family hovered over her, to no avail. She simply could not go on and prayed to die.

One day an elderly Christian lady came to see her. Silver head bent, eyes filled with care, the woman sat by the girl's bed. She never said much. She just held the clenched young fist in her strong, gnarled hand, gently rubbing each finger. Melissa began to relax. Tears streamed down the older woman's face as she felt the pain. A silent prayer went up. A current of love flowed between them.

She rose to leave, then placed a small gift-wrapped box near the girl's bed. "My dear, this will help."

The door softly closed. Melissa gingerly tugged on a brightly colored ribbon and opened the box. Inside lay a puzzle with no picture to go by. The pieces were worn from hard use.

Melissa began, hesitantly, then determined, alone with her thoughts. Hours passed unnoticed. Along with the puzzle came the older woman's answered prayer: the presence of the Lord repairing the girl's crushed life.

Piece by piece, God whispered direction, gently untangling and strengthening her life's confused, broken chunks and splinters. He soothed and healed wounds as He and Melissa worked hand in heart.

Several days passed. Both puzzles, life and picture,

were fitting together. New joy came to Melissa when she placed the last missing piece—and revealed the face of Christ.

The Lord is nigh unto them
that are of a broken heart;
and saveth such as be of a contrite spirit.
Psalm 34:18, KJV

BURNED OUT

Lord, I let myself get caught up in doing too many things. I'm burned out, so burned out I don't want to go anywhere or do anything. Bitterness and resentment are creeping in. Forgive me, Lord, and heal me. During this time of weakness, let me wait on You. Renew my strength, Lord, that I too can mount like the eagle. Please clip my wings just a little to keep me nearer You, to learn my limitations.

Let me put Your will first in my life, not the will of others. Give me the strength to say, "No thank you," in a loving, but firm way. Help me not to feel guilty. Perhaps I'm cheating others from the chance to serve.

Grant me wisdom in setting the right priorities: You first, my family second, and others next. Somewhere in there show me how to take time for me.

You are the Holy One of my life. I wonder, as You run an entire universe, how can You be concerned

81

with the likes of me? I praise You, O Lord, that You consider me a treasure and that You love me with Your unconditional and everlasting love.

Give me time to mend. In Your own time, send me forth to work again for You. But for now, help me to lie back and absorb your healing strength.

RESTING IN HIS WAY

When my weary body fails me,
And my mind is filled with strife,
When the world is pressing 'round me,
And I cannot deal with life,

When I've taken on the burdens,
Far more than I should share,
I cry with broken spirit,
"Lord, don't others even care?"

In my darkest midnight hours,
I hear You calmly say,
"You must take My yoke upon you.
You must rest within My way."

Then my many cares I gather,
And I lay them at Your feet.
Where I let Your love surround me,
As my every need You meet.

82

❑❑❑

But they that wait upon the Lord shall renew their strength; they shall mount up with wings as eagles; they shall run, and not be weary; and they shall walk, and not faint.

Isaiah 40:31, KJV

HUG THE LITTLE GIRL WITHIN ME

Dear Lord, hug the little girl within me—the little girl mistreated and abused. Encircle me with Your everlasting arms. Still my silent sobs. Anoint my head with Your healing oil; free me from nightmares of memories. Touch my scars with Your healing stripes. Soothe each muscle that suffered in anger and pain. I know You suffered, too. Piece together my broken heart. Your heart bled and You died for me. In sleepless nights, wrap me in Your comforting presence. Let me rest in the shadow of You, the Almighty. Hug the little girl in me as You cover me with Your feathers like a mother hen does her chicks. I find refuge under Your wings. Help me to face yesterday (wrong as it was), to forgive as You forgive me, and to look toward tomorrow with hope. Your faithfulness will be my shield and rampart. Let me not feel terror by night nor arrows that fly by day. Take my weakness and grant me Your strength. Make my feet swift at the dawning of a new day to do service for You. I go now in praise.

But please, Lord, don't ever stop hugging me.

From birth, Sandra had been repeatedly abused. No one else knew about it. Physical and emotional hurt became almost unbearable. God helped her. He provided friends who led Sandra to accept Christ as her Savior. Teachers, even strangers watered the seed of salvation as she grew up.

After high school, Sandra moved away, but couldn't be free from hurt and anger. God helped her again.

One Sunday she went to a nearby church. The people showed her the love she so desperately needed. Sandra's new pastor and wife spent hours of prayer and Bible study with Sandra and she learned to give hurts and bitterness to God. In spite of her parents not showing remorse for their actions she was learning to forgive. Yet the pain returned.

Sandra went with some friends to a women's retreat. Between conferences she slipped away to a prayer chapel and met with the Lord again. She told Him she couldn't continue with the hurt and grief any longer. In the chapel Sandra prayed that God would remove it all. He reminded her He was her Heavenly Father; that He loved the fragile little girl within her. Then He did something wonderful. Sandra felt like He reached down and wrapped His arms around her, rocking her back and forth while she sobbed out all her bad experiences. She knew He listened and took them all on His shoulders.

Although the past would never be right, Sandra accepted God's comfort and healing. She found peace. When pain and bad memories returned, she gave them back to the Lord, her Healer and Heavenly Father.

Read Psalm 91.

Part 7
TRIALS

A Shelter in the Time of Storm

The Lord's our Rock, in Him we hide—
A shelter in the time of storm;
Secure whatever ill betide—
A shelter in the time of storm.

O Rock divine, O refuge dear—
A shelter in the time of storm;
Be Thou our helper ever near—
A shelter in the time of storm.

Vernon J. Charlesworth

"As sure as God puts His children into the furnace of affliction, He will be with them in it."

Charles Spurgeon

Thou art my hiding place;
thou shalt preserve me from trouble;
thou shalt compass me about
with songs of deliverance. Selah.
Psalm 32:7, KJV

But the Lord is my defense;
and my God is the rock of my refuge.
Psalm 94:22, KJV

WONDERFUL GRACE OF JESUS

Wonderful, the matchless grace of Jesus,
Deeper than the mighty rolling sea.

Haldor Lillenas

And there arose a great storm of wind, and the waves
beat into the ship, so that it was now full. And he was
. . . asleep on a pillow: and they awake him, and say
unto him, Master, carest thou not that we perish?"
And he arose and rebuked the wind, and said unto the
sea, "Peace, be still." And the wind ceased, and there
was a great calm.

Mark 4:37–39, KJV

SINGING IN THE STORMS

The storms of life surround me, but I will not be tossed to and fro. I am anchored in Your steadfast love. A song of praise wells up from my heart. I will sing praise and glory to Your name, while You carry me through this, another storm. You alone know the answers and the outcome. I take comfort in Your mighty presence.

I turn into the wind, unafraid, ready to face each day head on, flanked with Your power and wisdom. In the peak of the storm, when I feel I can hold on no longer, I will call on Your name for peace. I will trust in You and will not feel afraid, as I nestle into Your protecting hands.

How is it that You have such mighty power, that the tempests in my life cease their crashing winds at Your command? How is it that You can calm my raging seas of circumstances and emotions and bring my life into Your control with Your powerful, yet hushed voice?

Even now, I hear Your whisper, "Peace, be still. Know I am Your God."

When the storm subsides, my song of praise for You will echo throughout the ages from generation to generation, telling of Your mighty works and deeds.

Thank You, dear Lord, for Your help and peace.

Two years ago, Dad and I took a trip to Quebec. Armed with video camera, munchies, and suitcases we headed out.

We found Quebec to be charming and lovely, but the little French we knew made following directions challenging. One night we had a motel reserved outside Montreal. The big city traffic and a storm warning for early afternoon concerned me. We planned to reach our destination by 3:00 P.M.

As we approached the outskirts of Montreal, we came onto major road construction. Exit signs had been removed and we missed our turnoff and ended up in downtown Montreal. I couldn't get us back to where we belonged. Time ticked away to 3:30. Rush hour traffic and the predicted storm came.

I strained to focus through rapid windshield wipers and the worst torrent of rain I'd ever seen. Gushing water prevented any vision beyond the hood of the car. There was no place to pull off and park. We had to keep moving! Trucks flew by on both sides, bathing the little car. Dad dug out his camera, recording the action. He always had loved a storm.

"Hey!" shouted Dad, "I can see clearly through this camera. It's like a filter."

I trusted Dad as he calmly directed me. We reached a traffic jam in a nearby tunnel. We stopped and I slumped over the wheel. I tried to appear calm for Dad's sake, but I was almost in tears.

Please, Lord, *I prayed*. Move the storm and help us find our way. *Traffic slowly edged on. The song,*

"Wonderful Grace of Jesus" whirred through my mind like a revolving tape. We approached the tunnel's opening and the sheet of rain. I nosed the car out. At the same time a gust of wind moved the storm to our right like the parting of the Red Sea. Before long we made it to our destination.

□□□

At times I find myself struggling and losing my way. I end up in one of life's storms. Then I remember Montreal. God doesn't always move or end the storms, but He calms my spirit, and He gives me a song for courage. Just like Dad's camera filtered through the rain, God filters through my problems. As I obey Him and read His word, He guides me along life's freeways.

□□□

LEARNING TO LET GO

Dear Father, I have done all I can to help. Yet I see my loved one's unwise decisions. I know I need to let go, but my love makes it impossible. Are You teaching me that by letting go I can show even greater love?

I realize my helplessness in solving another's problems. So, Lord, I place this one of mine in Your hands. I know You love each of us more than we can imagine. My dear one is no exception.

Grant me strength to stand up for what is right but to keep on loving. When unkind remarks hurt, let me not turn away, but merely step aside and give some space. Help me not to take the problems back by manipulating, fixing, or condemning, but to lend words of encouragement.

Teach me to be a comforter, not a crutch; to care, not to control; to listen, not demand my own way; and to cherish the good moments of each day.

I will not grieve for the past, but look to the future in hopeful anticipation.

Father, thank You for taking my fear and replacing it with Your pure love. Protect us with Your angels and guide with Your Spirit, that we will not fall to evil and harm.

❑❑❑

Darla and Sam struggled to raise their three teen-agers the right way. Although the parents loved the Lord, their efforts seemed futile. Their kids were breaking away from Christian teachings and heading for a life of disaster.

Darla felt devastated. She tried to hang onto them, bridging the gap (she thought) between them and God, one hand gripping God's and the other, her children.

One night after an argument, Darla stumbled to her bedroom and fell to her knees. Between sobs she revealed her broken heart to God.

"I can't lose my kids from You, Lord." She pounded the bed with her fists. "What more can I do?"

God's Spirit ministered to Darla with His love. He asked who came first, Him or her children? Would she be willing to go to Heaven with or without them? He told Darla to keep loving her kids, but to let them go. One by one Darla released her grip on her kids. She stood, feeling victory and relief. Then she realized when she finally let go, God was there to catch them in His everlasting arms. She had freed Him to work directly in their lives. Until then, she had been standing between them and the Lord.

Soon after, the children grew closer to Him. Now Darla and Sam thank the Lord for His help.

. . . and underneath are the everlasting arms . . .
Deuteronomy 33:27, KJV

PART 8
DELIVERANCE

CONSTANTLY ABIDING

There's a peace in my heart that the world
    never gave,
A peace it cannot take away,
Tho' the trials of life may surround like a cloud,
I've a peace that has come there to stay!

All the world seemed to sing of a Saviour
    and King
When peace sweetly came to my heart;
Troubles all fled away and my night turned to day.
Blessed Jesus, how glorious Thou art!

Constantly abiding, Jesus is mine;
Constantly abiding, rapture divine;
He never leaves me lonely,
whispers oh, so kind:
"I will never leave thee." Jesus is mine.

Mrs. Will L. Murphy

> . . . God has said,
> "Never will I leave you;
> never will I forsake you."
> So we say with confidence,
> "The Lord is my helper; I will not be afraid. . . ."
> Hebrews 13:5–6, NIV

I DON'T LIKE MY JOB

Dear Father, I pray You will help me with my job. Things aren't going right. I dread going to work and I need Your direction. On days I feel I'm doing more than my share, may my attitudes be right. Give me wisdom, I pray. When I do menial tasks, help me remember when Your Son, though King of Kings, came down from Heaven and often acted as a servant. Let me not be too proud to serve.

Help me to be honest in estimating my own abilities, to not put myself down or become a braggart. Teach me to appreciate a job well done, to feel an inner sense of accomplishment. I lean on You, not only on my skills. I know I can earn my pay and make a living; or I can give of myself and make a life.

Go before me when there is friction and backbiting. Let my motives be pure and uplifting, depending on Your help, so Your light can shine through.

❑❑❑

Whatever you do, work at it with all your heart,
as working for the Lord, not for men,
since you know that you will receive
an inheritance from the Lord as a reward.
It is the Lord Christ you are serving.
Colossians 3:23–24, NIV

*Work days lengthened to an endless grind for Candice.
Each time she heard her co-workers carelessly swear
and toss out dirty jokes, it pierced her heart like a
sword. She often felt she had to carry her load and part
of others' who weren't doing their share. Candice had
always cared for the people she worked with. Now she
was responding with sharp words and a critical attitude. She knew things were way off balance when she
saw the hurt in their eyes.*

*One afternoon as Candice read her Bible,
Colossians 3:23–24 seemed to jump out and speak to
her. She realized she had been focusing on her problems instead of the Lord.*

*A thought came so clearly it seemed almost audi-
ble:* The next time someone begins swearing, telling a
dirty joke, or not sharing the workload, stop and
quickly, quietly pray for that person. Try to understand and love each one.

God loves unconditionally. I must, too, *she realized.* When things get tough, Lord, please guard my attitude.

The next day Candice prayed for her co-workers. It wasn't long until she saw a big change. Mutual respect developed between her and others. Were they the ones who changed, or had she? Problems still came from time to time, but God continued to help through love and prayer.

FROM FEAR TO FAITH

Father, this crazy, out-of-control world seems to be getting worse all the time. We are pressed in with problems, crime, uncertainty, and fear on every side. What does my future hold, or the future of those I love and pray for? Will there even be a future? Am I too fearful to comprehend the what-if's? I am overwhelmed.

You promised You would never leave or forsake me. I know You are holding my hand each day, gently leading me through the good times and the bad.

O Lord, nothing can separate me from Your love. Not death, not life. Surely not the angels. Even the powers of hell cannot keep Your love from me. Today's fears and tomorrow's worries are needless in light of Your divine love. If I am on the highest mountain, in the air, on the water, or under the deepest ocean, nothing can ever separate me from You. My spirits soar like the eagle; You're there. They sink to the lowest despair. Still I know You are with me, showing Your magnificent love. Thank You for the love that Your Son, Jesus Christ, demonstrated, when He died on the cross for me so many years ago.

Thank You for Your promise that You will shine Your glorious light upon me. As I focus on You, O Lord, I know You are leading me forward. Thank You for Your goodness shining through me, Your shield before me, Your glory a protection around me. Thank You for guiding me with Your wisdom and counsel, now and in all my years to come. Someday, by Your grace, I will get to praise You forever in Heaven.

I'm ready to let You change my fear to faith. I place my hand in Yours and look forward with great expectation to the future You have prepared for me.

◻◻◻

Fear not this world's evil, neither envy those who do wrong and profit, when you do not. Those who refuse to trust Me will wither like parched grass and wilted plants. They shall fade to nothing.

I am always watching over you, no matter where you are or how difficult times may be for you. There is no limit to My power as I help you.

Trust Me and do My will. Be refreshed in My pastures. Know that I keep you safely in My care. Delight in Me. Commit your will to Mine. I will take the righteousness I have instilled within you and make it shine like the noonday sun!

Quiet yourself before Me and wait upon My direction. Flee from fighting and anger. Never seek revenge. Pray for those who misuse you. I am your God. I will fight the battles for you. You will be blessed with good times as you hope and trust in Me; and you will enjoy My peace that passes all understanding. You are my child and I am your God. (Psalm 37, paraphrased)

And we know that all things work together
for good to them that love God,
to them who are the called
according to his purpose.
Romans 8:28, KJV

❏❏❏

Hope in the Lord

Be of good courage,
He shall strengthen you.
Hope in the Lord,
He will see you through.

❏❏❏

Be strong and take heart,
all you who hope in the Lord.
Psalm 31:24, NIV

FROM CALAMITY TO CALM

Father, this day has too much responsibility for me. My head spins with frustration. My life is full of calamity. Help me to gain Your perspective. When my footing begins to slip, let me cling to You, my Fortress. Instill Your direction in my cluttered mind. When I am weak, lend me Your quiet, confident strength; when impatient, grant me Your patience. If I fail, help me not to keep punishing myself, but to leave it in Your hands and go on.

Teach me to eliminate those things that are unnecessary and to concentrate on the essentials. Help me slow down enough to take time for myself and You.

Keep my thoughts accurate, my hands sure, and my feet swift in doing Your will. Remind me of my limitations, Lord. Keep my step close behind—not in front—of You and protect me with Your strong hands.

At the day's end, I will lie down and reflect on all I have learned. I will recall how much You have helped me. I will praise You with great joy as I drift to sleep nestled in the protection of Your mighty wings.

❏❏❏

I will instruct you and teach you
in the way you should go;
I will counsel you and watch over you.
Psalm 32:8, NIV

❏❏❏

It's easy in our fast-paced world to let life control our schedules. Before long we find our days filled with jumble, wasted time, an overabundance of television, senseless actions, going nowhere. Like spinning wheels on a slippery freeway, we lose our spiritual footing, become irritable and frustrated. Our songs of praise and worship (when we listen to them) ring in our ears like fast-forward recordings. No concept. No application. No direction.

We need to pull off life's fast lane for awhile and turn to God for direction and strength. Let's tune in to His voice and marvel as He prepares the way for us. As we seek His direction, He miraculously makes more time in our day. Then at night we can look back and be satisfied within His will.

PART 9
FAMILY

HAPPY THE HOME WHEN GOD IS THERE

Happy the home when God is there,
And love fills every breast;
When one their wish, and one their prayer,
And one their heavenly rest.

Happy the home where Jesus' name
Is sweet to every ear,
Where children early lisp His fame,
And parents hold Him dear.

Happy the home where prayer is heard,
And praise is wont to rise,
Where parents love the sacred Word,
And all is wisdom prize.

Lord, let us in our homes agree,
This blessed peace to gain;
Unite our hearts in love to Thee,
And love to all will reign. Amen.

Henry Ware, Jr.

OUR NEWBORN BABY

Look at our beautiful baby, Lord, at these tiny fingers wrapped around mine. Look how this darling rests securely in my arms. See Daddy's proud gaze. Already my heart overflows with love. I talked to and prayed for this sweet one even while the baby was yet still in my womb.

What does our baby's future hold? Prepare the way that our child may grow up to love and serve You. Grant my husband and me wisdom in raising such a precious gift.

Today, O Lord, I dedicate our baby as a love offering to You. Like Hannah in days of old, I thank You for giving our little one to us. Here and now, I present our child at Your altar to be raised for Your service.

Let Your angels encamp around and about, and protect from evil and harm. Help us teach Your ways by truth and example. When we err, I pray, dear Lord, that You will help meet the needs and forgive us. Place Christians in life's pathway. I pray that You will create a special hunger in this little heart to know, love, and serve You completely.

Help me remember our child is lent to us for a little while and that You are the lender. Let me not take our dear one back from You or pursue my own ways outside Your will.

I will bless Your name, O Lord, thanking You for this wonderful infant gift. I praise Your name in my thoughts, motives, and actions forever.

But as for me and my household,
we will serve the Lord.
Joshua 24:15, NIV

The Lord bless you
and keep you;
the Lord make His face shine upon you
and be gracious to you;
the Lord turn His face toward you
and give You peace.
Numbers 6:24–26, NIV

THANK YOU FOR THIS SPECIAL DAY

Lord, I collapse onto our couch, kick my shoes off, and think of today's blessings. Family and friends bustled around. Children chattered with youthful excitement. Steaming irresistible foods simmered in the kitchen. Men exchanged stories and (thank You, Lord) helped with the little ones. It seems a whooshing dream; the day went so fast.

I reflect briefly on the struggles we've all had, the mountains we've fearfully conquered with Your help. Still we're together, loving and sharing. It was worth listening to each other and finding Your will through the years.

I'm tired, but I loved it all. At nightfall, little arms wrapped around my neck with an "I love you, Nana." Strong embraces from sons so dear and tender hugs from loving daughters filled my heart with joy. When did I earn such love and honor? I don't know, but I thank You for it, Lord. I treasure the look of pleasure and pride, the squeeze of a hand from my own dear parents.

Now the silence is here, ringing its tranquil melody. I lean over and nuzzle my head on my husband's shoulder. His look is one of fulfillment and approval. Love softly drifts between us.

I thank You, Lord, for this day that You created and for the love of family and friends.

As special days end in all their wild flurry, I'm often reminded of the true value in it all: not food, fancies, and elaborations, but my dearest friends and loved ones.

She watches over
the affairs of her household
and does not eat the bread of idleness.
Her children arise and call her blessed;
her husband also, and he praises her:

"Many women do noble things,
but you surpass them all."
Proverbs 31:27–29, NIV

BLESS THROUGH GENERATIONS

Father, in this uncertain world filled with danger and turmoil, I ask You to protect my family.

Will I live to see my children grown? Will I live to see my grandchildren? My great-grandchildren? I can only trust and make each day count for something.

Forgive us for providing such a world as this with all its problems. Yet I praise You for the many good things that are available to my children.

Lord, please bless my family for generations to come. May the Christian teachings we instill be passed from one generation to the next. Grant each dear one wisdom and strength.

Can it be that my simple prayers for them will be generated by Your power, the same power released when Your Son died on the cross and rose again? Will these prayers be made ageless? I take comfort that when I am gone, my prayers will continue into eternity with You, Lord Jesus, interceding on behalf of each one.

Just as You prayed for me in the garden of Gethsemane, I am assured that You accept my prayers for these, my children, my children's children, and on through the generations. I have no fear for their future, because I place them in Your loving care.

Thank You for Your peace.

❑❑❑

I pray for them. I am not praying for the world, but for those you have given me, for they are yours. All I have is yours, and all you have is mine. And glory has come to me through them. I will remain in the world no longer, but they are still in the world, and I am coming to you. Holy Father, protect them by the power of your name—the name you gave me—so that they may be one as we are one.

John 17:9–11, NIV

❑❑❑

Many families are tracing their heritages and genealogies. Some even take extra care to record interesting stories from days gone by. Hours are spent going through old family pictures, copying and preserving them for future generations.

This is good, but what are we doing to record the sacred spiritual lessons learned from our forefathers? The things they have learned and taught are more valuable than all the wealth and prestige in the world. I'm fortunate to have a wonderful Christian mother and father-in-law. I've gained insight and wisdom from them that I can apply and pass on.

Now I'm the grandparent. Some jokingly call me "senior citizen." Growing older seems to go synonymously with wisdom. Some who are younger don't seem to realize that all this so-called wisdom takes a lifetime to acquire through a slow, painful process. It is never-ending until we die.

Like many Christian parents and grandparents, my husband and I are extremely concerned about how our children, grandchildren, and great-greats to come through the years will handle life in this complex, troubled world. I thought a great deal about what I could do to help.

One of the most important things is to offer a prayer of dedication for our descendants. Remember Jesus' prayer had power, as do those we offer to God. When we are gone, the power of our prayers will continue.

Next, I decided to keep a spiritual journal. I also record a lot of scriptural lessons in the front and back of my Bible and in the margins. When my last Bible wore out, I spent the next year transferring my notes to my new Bible. I passed the old one to our oldest son and his wife. I hope through the generations it may still help some of our dear ones as it did me.

Times change. People may not. We still have the same needs and always will. God doesn't change. He still remains to help us. Recently I've been reading some valuable inspirational books written in the late 1800s and early 1900s. I was surprised at how many of the lessons in them still apply today.

Time is short. I am learning to weigh the important things and make time to follow through with them. It's worth an eternity.

PART 10

LOVE

LOVE DIVINE, ALL LOVES EXCELLING

Love divine, all loves excelling,
Joy of heaven, to earth come down,
Fix in us Thy humble dwelling,
All Thy faithful mercies crown.

Jesus, Thou art all compassion,
Pure, unbounded love Thou art;
Visit us with Thy salvation;
Enter every trembling heart.

Charles Wesley

Dear Friends, since God so loved us, we also ought to love one another. No one has ever seen God; but if we love one another, God lives in us and his love is made complete in us. There is no fear in love. But perfect love drives out fear. . . .We love because he first loved us. . . . And he has given us this command: Whoever loves God must also love his brother.

1 John 4:11–12, 18, 19, 21, NIV

HELP US START OVER

Lord, when did it change, this marriage of ours? When did we begin falling out of love? He used to give me flowers. I used to make his favorite dish. He used to say I was pretty. I used to wear his favorite dress. He used to touch my hair. I used to rub his back. We used to make special time for each other. A squeeze of the other's hand three times sent a magic, silent message, "I love you." What a priceless treasure, our love. Now, it's slipping through our fingers, perhaps never to return.

If there is even a glimmer of love, I don't know where it is. Yet, no matter how small, You, Lord, can find it.

Shield us from negative influences. Wrap us in your protective arms. Keep us from temptation to do wrong.

Helps us start over. Fan that tiny flame of love and help it grow. Let us remember that no matter how suave or eloquent we sound to others, it's all a clanging noise if we no longer share our love for each other. We can be wise and give all the best advice to our friends; but without love, it doesn't amount to anything.

Lord, teach us patience and kindness, even when things aren't going right. Teach us thoughtfulness. Help us put our marriage ahead of things pressing in on our lives. Show us how to build one another up instead of competing. Let us be willingly inconvenienced for one another's needs and quick to go the second mile, then the third. Calm our emotions that we may be slow to anger. Teach us to compliment and praise, to overlook times when the other messes up, to release childish, selfish attitudes.

Help us protect, not neglect; trust, not dishonor. Grant us strength to persevere in finding our lost love before it is too late. Even when our love fails, Yours never fails. Let Your love shine through us.

Fan our glimmer, Lord, and I will begin with three squeezes of my beloved's hand and an "I love you."

KEEP LOVING

Keep loving because of.
Keep loving in spite of.
Keep loving when to love is most difficult.
Keep loving when you have no strength.
Keep loving because Jesus loves you
in good times and bad
on mountain tops, in valleys.
When all else fails,
keep on loving.

A friend loveth at all times. . . .
Proverbs 17:17, KJV

THANK YOU FOR THE MAN I LOVE

He gazes at me from across the packed room. We're at just another meeting but I dressed to look my best. Do I see the same twinkle in his eyes I saw when we first met? Do I see the same look he wore on our wedding day? Am I so blessed that he still gazes at me with the same love and pride? Thank You, Lord, for that look. Thank You for today and for him.

Help me show to him the same love and thoughtfulness as when we first married. In our hurried schedules, let us look for time to spend with each other. Sometimes I love even sharing a second glass of iced tea on the patio at sundown.

I think of changes we've faced and will continue to experience. We have fallen in love with each other over and over again, even while changing.

Teach us to keep respecting one another's feelings. Teach us to put each other first, after You.

And, Lord, help me keep myself in a way that he will always look across the room with love and pride.

And now these three remain:
faith, hope and love.
But the greatest of these is love.
1 Corinthians 13:13, NIV

Love? I will tell you what it is to love!
It is to build with human hearts a shrine,
Where hope sits brooding like a beauteous dove,
Where time seems young, and life a thing divine.

Charles Swain

Thank You for My Friend

She was there, again, right when I needed a listening ear and a shoulder to lean on. Thank You for my friend, Lord. She is so special to me. Whenever we can't see each other, there are little thought waves going back and forth between us and little "arrow prayers" going up for one another during the day.

Thank You for my friend when she brings over a tray of cookies and I pour the tea. Amidst the work, our world stops while we take a little time for each other's company.

Help me never to take my friend for granted but to treat her with thoughtfulness. Help me to recognize when she wants my company and when she needs time alone.

I know we will remain close friends for many years to come. For every year we have, I am thankful.

A friend loves at all times . . .
A man of many companions may come to ruin,
but there is a friend who sticks closer than a brother.
Proverbs 17:17, 18:24, NIV

❑❑❑

True friendship stretches across continents and oceans
or is right next door. It has no geographic boundaries,
nor is its love measurable.

Thoughtful notes,
phone calls,
selfless actions
create warm, happy memories that last a lifetime.

To be and have a true friend in the fair and foul
weather of life makes us the wealthiest people on earth.

Part 11

God's
Faithfulness

I will sing of the mercies of the Lord for ever: with my mouth will I make known thy faithfulness to all generations. For I have said, Mercy shall be built up for ever: thy faithfulness shalt thou establish in the very heavens. I have made a covenant with my chosen, I have sworn unto David my servant, Thy seed will I establish for ever, and build up thy throne to all generations. Selah

O Lord God of hosts,
who is a strong Lord like unto thee?
or to thy faithfulness round about thee?
Psalm 89:1–4, 8 KJV

THE REBELLIOUS CHILD

Father, help my rebelling child. I am overwhelmed with worry. Have I raised this child, once little and carefree, to have this happen? Will my dear one's mistakes cause a lifetime of suffering? Is it all or partly my fault?

Forgive me, O Lord, for the wrongs I have caused my dear child. Let me humble myself and ask this loved one's forgiveness. Let me offer no excuses. Cleanse my heart from bitterness and give me a pure, unconditional love. Grant me wisdom. Teach me when to be lenient, when to be firm. Help me that my motives will be pure, honest, and aboveboard. Remind me often not to try fixing things.

Place Your angels about my child. Protect from sin and harm, and lead to Your perfect will. Soften our hearts. Give us both a hunger to love and serve You.

Now, dear Lord, I release control of my beloved child to You. I will trust You in every situation and timing. Even when I don't understand why, still will I trust and praise You. Through these troublesome times I know You are helping and keeping my dear one in Your care.

Thank You for victories to come. Thank You for hearing my prayers. Thank You that You can go places with my child that I can't. As the answers to prayer come, may I write them down and remember them. Praise You, O God, for Your mighty works. In You I put my total trust.

❑❑❑

Above all, love each other deeply,
because love covers over a multitude of sins.
1 Peter 4:8, NIV

Praise the Lord, O my soul;
    all my inmost being, praise his holy name.
Praise the Lord, O my soul,
    and forget not all his benefits.
He forgives all my sins
    and heals all my diseases;
he redeems my life from the pit
    and crowns me with love and compassion.
He satisfies my desires with good things,
    so that my youth is renewed like the eagle's.
Psalm 103:1–5, NIV

. . . Blessed is the man who trusts in the Lord,
    whose confidence is in him.
He will be like a tree planted by the water
    that sends out its roots by the stream.
Jeremiah 17:7–8, NIV

117

My husband Bob and I have five sons, now fine grown men. When we reflect on their teenage years, we recall many happy memories, but also some frightening moments.

During the rebellious, emotional ping-pong times we discovered valuable lessons. First, we learned to hold a steady, consistent course so our kids could have something stable to look toward. If we strayed in the slightest, it magnified in our children. They scrutinized and challenged everything we said and did.

As our children attempted to find their own way, they tested us for purity and validity. No amount of speeches or attempts to set them straight worked. Communication, listening, and love helped most. We also soon discovered our example meant much more than mere words.

Another lesson learned was to maintain a close fellowship with our Lord. He was our Guide, our Counselor, Friend, and source of strength. Because of this we were able to give and regive each child to God. He could go with them where we couldn't and speak to each one when our words didn't reach them.

Now we praise God for His miracles and answered prayers and for our beloved family. We still hold those six-foot sons, our precious daughters by marriage, and now our grandchildren up to God and leave them in His care each day.

After Julie's husband left, she felt helpless and alone; meanwhile, her teenage son Tony was going through rocky times. Julie worried for him and prayed for God's help.

One afternoon they decided to walk to the river. Julie loved these long walks and talks she and Tony took, just the two of them. Warm sunlight cast sparkling reflections on the water, sending glittering flashes to the nearby trees.

"This is my favorite spot, Mom." Tony motioned toward a grassy patch and a nearby tree that bent precariously over the riverbank. "And this is what I like to do. Watch me!" With one great lunge, Tony was airborne and grabbed a low branch. Inch by inch, hand over hand, he worked his way out over the rushing current.

Julie gasped. "Is that tree strong enough to hold you?"

The rubbery branch swayed from Tony's slim body. "Sure, Mom. Its roots sink deeper than the tree is tall."

Julie sat on the soft emerald turf and watched her son. She pondered her worries for him. She knew God had given this walk as a reminder to sink her roots of prayer and Bible reading deep in the Lord, so He could help them.

After that when times got tough, she remembered their special walk by the river and God's strengthening roots. She knew they could make it through. Just the three of them—Julie, Tony, and Jesus.

FATHER, HEAR THE PRAYER WE OFFER

Father, hear the prayer we offer;
Not for ease that prayer shall be,
But for strength that we may ever
Live our lives courageously.

Not forever in green pastures
Do we ask our way to be,
But the steep and rugged pathway
May we tread rejoicingly.

Not forever by still waters
Would we idly quiet stay,
But would smite the living fountains
From the rocks along the way.

Be our strength in hours of weakness;
In our wanderings be our guide;
Through endeavor, failure, danger,
Father, be thou at our side.
Amen.

Love M. Willis

PART 12

CHALLENGE

"A CHARGE TO KEEP I HAVE"

A charge to keep I have,
A God to glorify;
A never dying soul to save,
And fit it for the sky.

To serve the present age,
My calling to fulfill
O may it all my powers engage
To do my Master's will!

Charles Wesley

However, I consider my life
worth nothing to me,
if only I may finish the race and
complete the task
the Lord Jesus has given me
the task of testifying to
the gospel of God's grace.
Acts 20:24, NIV

LET MY ROOTS SINK DEEP

Lord, I sit alone by a quiet stream. My thoughts turn to Psalm 23. The waters gently ripple by. Trees gracefully bow their branches and teasingly rustle their leaves in the pure, fresh breeze. A bird lilts a beckoning call to its mate. A distant falcon pierces the air with its echoing screech.

Peace. Thank You, Lord. But what about when I must return to the hustle and bustle? How can I be prepared?

I look at the trees; their roots sink deep by the stream. In the same way, let my roots sink deep into You. Let me feed on Your Word. As we commune in prayer, let me drink from the living water of Your spirit. Let me jump in and be bathed by Your cleansing power. I will rely on You rather than things that are shallow and temporary. I can't depend on my own abilities and strength, but I'm confident in Your care and direction.

I will take special notice of the good things when they come. I will fix my mind on what is pure and lovely and upright.

When the heat and winds of life's storms come, I will not fear; I know You are near. I will not worry but keep on producing a life that is a blessing for You and others.

Let me take time often to come drink from Your quiet stream. I thank You for it.

The Lord is my shepherd
     I shall not want.
He maketh me to lie down in green pastures:
     he leadeth me beside the still waters.
He restoreth my soul:
     he leadeth me in the paths of righteousness
     for his name's sake.

Yea, though I walk through the valley of the
     shadow of death,
I will fear no evil:
     for thou art with me;
thy rod and thy staff they comfort me.

Thou preparest a table before me in the
     presence of mine enemies:
thou anointest my head with oil;
     my cup runneth over.
Surely goodness and mercy shall follow me
     all the days of my life:
and I will dwell in the house of the Lord forever.

Psalm 23, KJV

Praising God from the Pits

Lord, I want to praise You from the pits. Not the pits of self-pity, but the pits carefully placed in the heart of life's race track. I don't have time to feel sorry for myself. I'm in the middle of a race for You.

Each time I round the bend, I trust You to run me through Your checklist to see if I'm in alignment and synchronized to Your will.

I know there are others watching me, but I also know You are helping me discard things and habits that would inhibit me.

I want to praise You as I run with determination. I will put forth every ounce of strength. At times I'm scorned and tested. Other times I'm tempted to take a side path, but I will keep my eyes turned to You, my Creator, the very Being of my faith. I remember how You were scorned, how You were tempted, how You shed Your blood and died on the cross for me.

So when I am weary, lift my hands that I might praise You from the pits. Strengthen my arms, I pray. Keep my feet swift and sure. Make each day's path level before me. My life, I give to You. With all my being, I run this race for You.

MOVING A MOUNTAIN A TEASPOONFUL AT A TIME

This mountain of mine is huge, Father! I've prayed over and over that You would remove it from me but still it remains, looming, threatening. Must I move it myself? I don't think I can handle such a task.

There's much to be done and so little time. Yet I am determined. Whether I'm weary or not, in season or out, I must begin moving my mountain, even if it's only a teaspoonful at a time.

Lord, help me face each problem head on within Your will. When fires and hot, parching winds surround me, remind me You are here. When fierce, storms assault me, help me dig in my heels and hang onto Your Word. When I'm forced to plod through sinful murk and mud, I ask You to cleanse me with Your pure, sweet living water. Lighten my step that I don't get bogged down in such things.

When evil seeks to devour me, I seek protection with Your holy armor. When others criticize me and self-righteously smirk at my mountain, I may feel crushed and defeated. Lift me up then, I pray. Help me hold my head high and go on. For I am Your child—the child of a King!

When life's heavy trees and rocks fall on and about me, I shall not fear, for You are helping, guiding all the way.

At times I may ask, "Why me, Lord? Why must I move this mountain and carry this tree, my cross? I'm too weak!" Please help me. Please love me. I trust You,

for this mountain shall be removed and I praise You for
the victories to come.

❏❏❏

Ignore the doubter.
   Remain strong.
Don't be afraid to fail.
   Keep your eye on the goal.
Maintain a realistic pace.
   Listen to the One who coaches you.

❏❏❏

Therefore, since we are surrounded by
such a great cloud of witnesses,
let us throw off everything that hinders
and the sin that so easily entangles,
and let us run with perseverance
the race marked out for us.
Hebrews 12:1, NIV

❏❏❏

Jesus looked at them and said,
"With man this is impossible,
but with God all things are possible."
Matthew 19:26, NIV

❏❏❏

Wouldn't it be wonderful if we could call on God and He would snap His fingers and make all our troubles disappear? It rarely works that way.

I'm reminded of how God works these things together for a purpose. I watch athletes train day after weary day, building their strength, preparing for competition. How proud they are of their improvements! I think of students who toil long and hard for degrees, or artists who paint landscapes, starting over and over until they're right.

What about disasters? Many thrown our way loom like mountains, but with God's help we can work through them all. Each time, we grow. We feel pride, strength, and satisfaction that we could never have experienced if all were handed to us on a silver platter.

There are reasons God lets us struggle. There are lessons to learn and lives to touch along the way. At times our mountains prepare us to help others.

When I watch the ants, I'm awed at the huge loads they carry, some far bigger than their bodies. They never give up, but keep struggling. When the load is too great, another ant often shows up. I wish I could reach down to help but I'm too big. Perhaps that's why God sends other Christians to help us. May they not idly stand by or criticize. God is working when another dear one picks up a teaspoon and pitches in.

The day comes when we look back at what we have accomplished with God's help in moving that mountain and carrying our cross. We can see ruts and furrows along the way. Where did they come from?

Surely we weren't strong enough to make them! Some have come from His almighty hand—and some were made when Jesus picked up our heavy cross and carried it for us.

❏❏❏

NEVER GIVE UP

When you
    believe you're crushed, you are.
    defy not the odds, you lose.
    claim not the victory, you fail.
    settle for one goal, you grow stagnant.

But when you
    learn from the struggles, you resolve.
    ignore the put downs, you grow.
    choose success, you soar.
    believe in yourself, you gain confidence.
    accept Christ, you gain strength.
    toil unceasingly, you achieve.
    press on, you are enriched.
    fall and start over, you win.

When you do all this, you shall gain life's prize.

I WILL NEVER GIVE UP

Lord, right now I feel helpless and alone. There appears to be no hope. Please, show me You are still near. People say my situation is a lost cause. Yet Your infinite wisdom and mercy continue to prove that You are near, helping me along the way, showing Your will. Even in troubled times my voice breaks out in song, praising You for Your power and forgiving mercy. No, I will never give up but seek You out day by day, hour by hour.

How many times have I disappointed You and pleaded for Your forgiveness? Your eternal love forgives me over and over.

When troubles surround me, I will not be afraid. In the midst of hopelessness, I feel Your helping hand. In spite of my failings, I know Your compassion and forgiveness. In the midst of my broken pride, I sense Your strength and comfort. In my loss of direction, I look to Your leading.

I thank You, already, for how You lift me from the depths of despair, how You help and heal, how You forgive and offer favor to last me all of my life.

I will always be secure in your protection. I won't be shaken. I will stand steadfast and sure. I will never give up. Thanks be to You, O Lord.

I press on toward the goal to win the prize
for which God has called me
heavenward in Christ Jesus.
Philippians 3:14, NIV

I Want to Leave My Mark for You

I know not what each day holds, or what time I have left to serve. This I do know, dear Lord, I want to leave my mark for You.

Help me make every day count. Remind me to lay aside my own wants, to be willingly inconvenienced and used for You. Let me not put anything before You, no matter how good it seems. Help me shed bad habits that slow me down from doing Your will.

I can only leave my mark for You by replacing idle time with purposeful movement. When I rest, I open my heart that You may fill me with Your strength and spirit.

Teach me to let go of yesterday, live fully today, and look with excitement toward tomorrow. I am awed as I daily come to know You more. I feel You shower love upon me like a refreshing summer rain.

Even though I am unworthy, I long to reach the end of life's journey and see You face to face. In the meantime, Lord, may I use each day, each hour, each moment to leave my mark for You. Amen.

PART 13

WORSHIP

THE CHURCH'S ONE FOUNDATION

The church's one Foundation
Is Jesus Christ her Lord;
She is His new creation
By water and the word;
From heaven He came and sought her
To be His holy bride;
With His own blood He bought her,
And for her life He died.

Elect from every nation,
Yet one o'er all the earth,
Her charter of salvation
One Lord, one faith, one birth;
One holy name she blesses,
Partakes one holy food,
And to one hope she presses,
With every grace endued.
Amen.

Samuel Sebastian Wesley

PRAISE YOU, THREE IN ONE

I love You, O Lord, my God, with all my heart, my soul, my strength. Never will I forget You, You are my *Father,* and I, Your child. There is not the slightest shadow of Your turning Your back on me.

How great You are as You order the beginning, the present, and even the future. How marvelous is Your wisdom.

What a miracle the angels and shepherd witnessed when You, the *Son of God,* came to earth as a tiny baby in a lowly manger. How amazing for Your Father's promises to be fulfilled. In a flash of time, You showed us how to mature from babe to manhood, how to grow in wisdom and stature, how to live a holy life as a young man—yet still be the Son of God.

In Your last days when You were with Your disciples, You tried to prepare them for what was to come. You were truly the appointed heir of the Father who created all things. In His brilliant image, You fulfilled God's promises.

My heart cries out to think of how You took all the world's sins on Yourself and became a living sacrifice. I can't comprehend how You went to hell, carried our sins to heaven, and placed all the wrongs we have ever done at the mercy seat of God! How can You love us so? How can You love me so?

To You be the glory as You reign in Heaven with our Father—our Father, because You adopted us into Your family. There You sit at the Father's right hand. To You, dear Jesus, be all glory and honor and praise.

Before Jesus left, He promised us You would come, *Holy Spirit.* Now I pray Your presence will abide with me in my heart throughout each day. Even as the Father and the Son, You, Holy Spirit, show me the way, the truth, and the life. You give me a peace and joy no other can provide. I cannot see You but I know Your presence: Your soft whispers, Your warnings, Your nudges, Your warm steadfast love. I know these things because You have seen fit to fill me to overflowing with Your precious Spirit.

I praise You, God, for still being with me, because You dwell within my heart. Thank You for Your loving kindness. You are my Father, my Savior, my Comforter. You, in all Your mercy, washed my sins away and saved me. After You made me clean, You filled me with a new life. Now I can live in Your grace and love. Through all my life will I commune and live in You, and You in me. All my days I will serve You. Praise be to You, O God!

❏❏❏

The grace of the Lord Jesus Christ,
and love of God,
and the communion of the Holy Ghost,
be with you all. Amen.
2 Corinthians 13:14, KJV

❏❏❏

Make a joyful noise unto the Lord, all ye lands.
Serve the Lord with gladness;
come before his presence with singing.
Know ye that the Lord he is God:
it is he that hath made us, and not we ourselves;
we are his people, and the sheep of his pasture.
Enter into his gates with thanksgiving,
and into his courts with praise;
be thankful unto him, and bless his name.
For the Lord is good; his mercy is everlasting;
and his truth endureth to all generations.
Psalm 100, KJV

❏❏❏

GLORIE PATRI

Glory be to the Father,
and to the Son,
and to the Holy Ghost;

As it was in the beginning,
is now, and ever shall be,
world without end.
Amen, Amen.

Traditional

YOUR CHURCH IS MY HAVEN

The world and its good and bad responsibilities press 'round on every side all week. I rush to keep up. My day of worship finally comes. I *still* rush, through Your sanctuary doors, striving to fulfill my service. In the hurry of it all, I often feel drained.

Now as I listen to the organ, I quiet my heart. Lord, it is good to drink from Your fountain of holiness. Though others are seated about me, I become unaware. I sense only the presence of Your Holy Spirit descending on a lowly one such as I, ministering, loving, teaching, and filling me to overflowing.

Thank You for my church, these loving people, the body of Christ. And thank You for quieting my heart so I may listen to You.

❑❑❑

I rejoiced with those who said to me,
    "Let us go to the house of the Lord."
Our feet are standing
    in your gates, O Jerusalem.

For the sake of my brothers and friends,
    I will say, "Peace be within you."
For the sake of the house of the Lord our God,
    I will seek your prosperity.

                     Psalm 122:1–2, 8–9, NIV

❑❑❑

WORSHIP IN SILENCE

I wait in silent worship, Lord Jesus. Mere words cannot utter my reverence for You, the one true God. You created the earth, the skies—and me. I'm glad I am Yours.

All blessings, honor, and power; might, glory, and wisdom; praise and thanksgiving I offer to You.

In silence, I give You praise and wait so You can minister to me.

I pray in Your name, amen.

BE STILL

"Be still," I hear Him softly say.
"Be still, lay all aside."
He who made the universe stoops down,
and gathers up my cares.

"Be still," He chides again.
His work begins within my weary soul.
"Be patient. In quiet stay.
Listen to me."

Though pressed on every side,
I clear my heart and mind.
In timid voice and heart,
I lift to Him my praise.

How quiet, His presence.
How healing, His words.
In hushed awe, I listen.
I savor each one.

My will, He bends.
My heart, He sweeps clean.
My strength, He renews.
My soul, He fills to overflowing.

He teaches through His word.
I heed what He tells me.
I stand and give Him praise.
Together we go forth to serve.

THE OCEANS OBEY YOU

Oh Lord, You are mightier than the huge breakers crashing against the ocean rocks. No other is greater than You! You display Your faithfulness in the cycle of the tides. How magnificent is the way their waves rise and fall at Your command. You shout and they rise. You whisper, they drift softly back into the ocean's depths. How do You cause the waters to stop at the shore? This water, soft as silk and harder than bricks, obeys Your will.

I walk along the sandy beach. I gaze out over the deep waters and recall the turbulence in my own life. Thank You for bringing my storms under control. Your mighty hand snatched me out of trials and tribulations; You have never dropped me.

As I stand gazing at Your marvelous creation, I dig my toes in the sand. The strong wind whips my hair. My tongue savors the salty air. I breathe deeply. Clean, cool air fills my lungs. Your refreshing Spirit surrounds me. You honor me with Your presence. I tremble at the thought of Your greatness.

Thank You for Your creation. Thank You, God, for life.

The Lord reigneth, he is clothed with majesty;
    the Lord is clothed with strength,
wherewith he hath girded himself:
    the world also is stablished,
that it cannot be moved.

Thy throne is established of old:
    thou art from everlasting.
The floods have lifted up, O Lord,
    the floods have lifted up their voice;
    the floods lift up their waves.
The Lord on high is mightier
    than the noise of many waters, yea,
    than the mighty waves of the sea.
Thy testimonies are very sure:
    holiness becometh thine house,
    O Lord, for ever.

Psalm 93, KJV

❑❑❑

SACRIFICE OF PRAISE

Father, I offer You my sacrifice of praise. Forever will I honor Your name. I lift my voice in song, giving You praise. In the morning I praise You for a new day. At evening, I rejoice in all You have done.

As long as I have breath, I will praise You. I give You my whole being, that it may be pleasing unto You and acceptable in Your sight. This is the least I can do for You, dear Lord.

I want to constantly praise You to my friends and loved ones so they, too, can know all You have done for me. I long for them to learn to know and love You and experience real joy.

No other is so worthy of my praise. You are power, wisdom, honor, glory, might, and blessing. Your words fill my life. Your lessons teach me wisdom. Let everything I do and say be pleasing unto You, so I may be a true reflection of You to others and glorify my Father, who is in heaven. Again, I offer the only thing I can give You, my sacrifice of praise. Praise be the Lord!

❑❑❑

How can I repay the Lord
    for all his goodness to me?
I will lift up the cup of salvation
    and call on the name of the Lord.
I will fulfill my vows to the Lord
    in the presence of all his people.

Precious in the sight of the Lord
    is the death of his saints.
O Lord, truly I am your servant;
    I am your servant, the son of your maidservant;
    you have freed me from my chains.

I will sacrifice a thank offering to you
    and call on the name of the Lord.
I will fulfill my vows to the Lord
    in the presence of all his people,
in the courts of the Lord—
    in your midst, O Jerusalem.
Praise the Lord.

Psalm 116:12–19

JOY OF THE LORD

My days are long and weary. My strength is almost gone. I lift my eyes to You, O Lord, my joy and strength. My heart quickens. New energy surges through my body. Gladness fills my heart as I concentrate on You.

Thank You for helping me focus on You, Lord, rather then the negative things in life. When the tasks I have to accomplish seem impossible, thank You for pumping new life into me. Truly, Lord, Your joy is my strength.

As I go about my duties, may Your joy radiate through me. Let Your light shine in me, Your servant, because of the good works You have done. I sing praises and am blessed with Your strength.

Only temporary happiness comes from this world. I take heart in Your joy, the joy of the Holy Spirit. It is indescribable, straight from Heaven! Your joy covers suffering, trials, sadness, and exhaustion.

When I experience it, my cup overflows. There is no situation so difficult I cannot overcome with pure, refreshing joy and strength from You. You refresh, cleanse, and comfort, exhilarate and encourage.

I rejoice again and again! You, Lord, stoop from Your throne in Heaven, reach down, and nourish me with the Water of Life. You wipe away my tears and replace them with gladness anew and Your pure, sweet joy.

. . . for the joy of the Lord is your strength.
Nehemiah 8:10, NIV

I'LL SING YOUR PRAISES

I'll sing Your praises all my days,
Though my rhythm may be slow,
In weary tune I lift my song,
Your Spirit I now know.

Lord, when life's shadows cross my sky,
And the sun is not in view,
I still sing out in faltering voice,
My praises unto You.

May I keep singing all my days,
Though my voice is stretched and thin,
The bubbling, joyous waters stir
From Your Spirit deep within.

Let others hear my singing, Lord.
Let Your glory ring out clear.
And may they say, "I too shall sing,
Throughout my span of years."

Sing to the Lord a new song,
>   his praise in the assembly of the saints.
Let Israel rejoice in their Maker;
>   let the people of Zion be glad in their King.
Let them praise his name with dancing
>   and make music to him with tambourine and
>   harp.
For the Lord takes delight in his people;
>   he crowns the humble with salvation.
Let the saints rejoice in this honor
>   and sing for joy on their beds.

Psalm 149:1–5, NIV

SAVING WORDS OF JESUS

Jesus, the words You uttered from the cross are so priceless. Thank You for keeping those promises true down through history, even to today.

When they came to the place called The Skull, there they crucified him, along with the criminals—one on his right, the other on his left. Jesus said, "Father, forgive them, for they do not know what they are doing."

Luke 23:33–34, NIV

Thank You for forgiveness.

Then he said, "Jesus, remember me when you come into your kingdom." Jesus answered him "I tell you the truth, today you will be with me in paradise."

Luke 23:42–43, NIV

Thank You for Paradise.

Near the cross of Jesus stood his mother, his mother's sister, Mary the wife of Clopas, and Mary Magdalene. When Jesus saw his mother there, and the disciple whom he loved standing nearby, he said to his mother, "Dear woman, here is your son," and to the disciple, "Here is your mother."

John 19:25–27, NIV

Thank You for caring.

From the sixth hour until the ninth hour darkness came over all the land. About the ninth hour Jesus cried out in a loud voice, "Eloi, Eloi, lama sabachthani?"—which means, "My God, my God, why have you forsaken me?"

Matthew 27:45–46, NIV

Thank You for bearing our sins.

Later, knowing that all was now completed, and so that the Scripture would be fulfilled, Jesus said, "I am thirsty."

John 19:28, NIV

Thank You for living water.

When he had received the drink, Jesus said, "It is finished." With that, he bowed his head and gave up his spirit.

John 19:30, NIV

Thank You for fulfilling
God's promise to save us.

Jesus called out with a loud voice, "Father, into your hands I commit my spirit."

Luke 23:46, NIV

Thank You for victory

THE SAVIOUR

Behold the Saviour of mankind
Nailed to the shameful tree;
How vast the love that Him inclined
To bleed and die for me.

Hark! how He groans, while nature shakes,
And earth's strong pillars bend!
The Temple's veil asunder breaks,
The solid marbles rend.

'Tis finished! now the ransom's paid,
"Receive My Soul" He cries;
See—How He bows His sacred head!
He bows His head and dies!

But soon He'll break death's iron chain,
And in full glory shine.
O Lamb of God! was ever pain—
Was ever love like Thine?

Samuel Wesley, Sr.

MY REFUGE AND MY STRENGTH

When troubles surround me, Lord, I will trust in You. Thank You for Your help whenever I come to You with my needs. I hide within Your cloak of safety. I take courage in Your strength. No matter what my situation, You are there guiding, helping.

When all seems impossible, You are my mighty deliverer. Even though I am unworthy, You perform marvelous wonders in my life.

Thank You for Your promises to supply all my needs. How grateful I am that You keep Your word. You, Lord, are all-knowing and constant. Heaven and earth will pass away. Grass and flowers will fade. Your word, dear Lord, will remain forever.

Thank You for being with me. Sometimes I feel weak. Yet when I'm at my lowest ebb, Your strength seems to show up the best. When I am in Your will, I can do all things You ask of me, through Your name, Christ Jesus. Thank You for granting me the strength I so often desperately need. This is because of Your mighty power working within me.

Alone, I amount to nothing. As I obey and serve You, others can see Your wondrous works within me. And You, my Lord, are the joy of my salvation, my refuge, and my strength. Praise be to You, O God.

GOD IS MY STRONG SALVATION

God is my strong salvation;
What foe have I to fear?
In darkness and temptation
My light, my help is near.
Though hosts encamp around me,
Firm in the fight I stand;
What terror can confound me,
With God at my right hand?

Place on the Lord reliance,
My soul, with courage wait;
His truth be thine affiance,
When faint and desolate.
His might thy heart shall strengthen,
His love thy joy increase;
Mercy thy days shall lengthen;
The Lord will give thee peace.

James Montgomery

God is our refuge and strength,
an ever present help in trouble.
Therefore we will not fear.
Psalm 46:1–2, NIV

AS LONG AS I HAVE BREATH

Praise You, O Lord. I praise You with all my soul. You are the Lord of my life. With all my heart will I sing praises unto Your holy name.

My hope is in You, my God, my help and strength. You who created the heaven, the earth, the sea, are everything. How grand is the way the earth rotates and tilts at Your command. I marvel at how You decide the count of stars and even know their names! How wonderful the way You blanket the earth with white snow and sprinkle frost about like glittering ashes. The earth rests. As life's icy winds blow, You speak again. At Your command, warm breezes cause the snow to melt and the waters to stir. You cloak the sky with Your clouds. You let Your blessings fall in droplets of rain. You change the brown grasses to emerald green. Their roots become strong. The cattle are nourished and strengthened. How great and powerful You are. How measureless Your understanding.

My hope isn't in the strength of earthly things that fail. Instead, my delight, my full trust and love are in You. I shall not put my confidence in people of high places, nor in any mortal. They can't grant me life eternal. Only You can, Lord. When my earthly life is over, my plans matter no more, but precious life with You remains.

When I'm oppressed, You hold me up. When I'm needy, You provide for me. When I feel trapped in troublesome situations, You set me free. When I'm lonely, You are my friend.

How wonderful it is to sing my praises to You. It seems so natural. My heart overflows with love for You. How could I ever ignore Your majestic ways? If all were to be silent, even the rocks would cry out and praise You. Let me always praise You, my Lord. As long as I have breath I will praise Your name.

I Look to You, Dear Lord

You are my hope, the Lord of my life. I wait on You and move cautiously in my decisions. I'm not ashamed to trust in Your guidance, Lord. Instead, I feel thankful for the encouragement and surety You give me. As I trust in You, I'm filled with peace. Throughout the day, my thoughts often turn to You for direction and strength. In quiet and confidence I find the strength only You can give.

You, dear Father, are my Rock and my Defender; I shall not fear. I know in whom I believe and I'm per-suaded You keep me close to You day by day.

I look to You, I doubt not in Your unfailing love for me. Thank You.

In Jesus' name, amen.

Praise the Lord.

How good it is to sing praises to our God,
　　how pleasant and fitting to praise him!

He determines the number of stars
　　and calls them each by name.
Great is our Lord and mighty in power;
　　his understanding has no limit.

He covers the sky with clouds
　　he supplies the earth with rain
　　and makes grass grow on the hills.
He provides food for the cattle
　　and for the young ravens when they call.

. . . the Lord delights in those who fear him,
　　who put their hope in his unfailing love.
Let everything that has breath praise the Lord.
　　Praise the Lord.
　　　Psalm 147:1, 2, 4–5; 147:8–9, 11; 150:6, NIV

O Lord, thou art my God;
I will exalt thee, I will praise thy name;
for thou has done wonderful things;
thy counsels of old are faithfulness and truth.

Thou wilt keep him in perfect peace,
whose mind is stayed on thee:
because he trusteth in thee.
Trust ye in the Lord for ever;
for in the Lord
JEHOVAH is everlasting strength.
Isaiah 25:1, 26:3–4, KJV

I LOOK TO YOU

I look to You, Jesus.
Your promises are true.
I love You, Lord Jesus.
You always see me through.

I walk with You, Jesus.
You gently speak to me.
I'll serve You, Lord Jesus,
Until Your face I see.

ALTHOUGH I'VE NEVER SEEN YOU

I love You, Lord. Even though I have never seen You, I still believe in You. I love You because I know You first loved me. Day by day I feel Your love. In You, I live and move and have my being.

I don't have to see You to believe. Your Holy Spirit is evidence enough. You saved me and are constantly guiding me and supplying my needs. How rich I feel! You are my only true hope in life. What joy I have in believing in You.

Without a doubt I will trust in You always.

❑❑❑

A week later his disciples were in the house again, and Thomas was with them. Though the doors were locked, Jesus came and stood among them and said, "Peace be with you!" Then he said to Thomas, "Put your finger here; see my hands. Reach out your hand and put it into my side. Stop doubting and believe."

Thomas said to him, "My Lord and my God!"

Then Jesus told him, "Because you have seen me, you have believed; blessed are those who have not seen and yet have believed."

John 20:26–29, NIV

YOUR ENDURING LOVE

Thank You, O Lord, for Your goodness and for Your enduring love. You are Lord of everything. Great are the wonders You perform. All You do is enveloped in Your love.

When You formed the earth and parted the waters, You created it all in love. When You made the sun to shine by day and the moon and stars for night, You had a plan. You separated darkness and light, summer and winter, springtime and fall. In wisdom You created it all. And in it all You showed Your magnificent love.

When all is well in my life, Your steadfast love is with me. When My life ebbs to its lowest estate, still Your love for me endures. When my enemies threaten me, You surround me with Your protection. You provide me with food and clothing. How grateful I am. I will praise You all my days for Your eternal, enduring love.

Give thanks to the Lord, for he is good.
　　His love endures forever.
Give thanks to the God of gods.
　　His love endures forever.
Give thanks to the Lord of lords:
　　His love endures forever.
To him who alone does great wonders,
　　His love endures forever.
Who by his understanding made the heavens,
　　His love endures forever.
Who spread out the earth upon the waters,
　　His love endures forever.
Who made the great lights—
　　His love endures forever.
The sun to govern the day,
　　His love endures forever.
The moon and stars to govern the night;
　　His love endures forever.

Psalm 136:1–9, NIV

THE EARTH IS YOURS

Father, everything on this earth is Yours. The entire world belongs to You. Thank You for how You created it and have control. Everything I enjoy, all that I have is Yours.

How sad it is to see some worship the mountains, the moon and stars, and everything that grows. It all came from You. How presumptuous of man not to recognize You as the bountiful Giver.

I praise You, Lord, for the beauty You loaned me on this earth. Although I'll only be here a short time, I pray for Your wisdom so I may responsibly care for this earth.

Thank You for all its beauty. Praise You for being Lord of it all.

The earth is the Lord's and everything in it,
    the world, and all who live in it;
for he founded it upon the seas
    and established it upon the waters.

Who may ascend the hill of the Lord?
    Who may stand in his holy place?
He who has clean hands and a pure heart,
    who does not lift up his soul to an idol
    or swear by what is false.

He will receive blessing from the Lord
    and vindication from God his Savior.
Such is the generation of those who seek him,
    who seek your face, O God of Jacob. Selah
                      Psalm 24:1–6, NIV

A gentle answer turns away wrath,
    but a harsh word stirs up anger.
The tongue of the wise commends knowledge,
    but the mouth of the fool gushes folly.
The eyes of the Lord are everywhere,
    keeping watch on the wicked and the good.
The tongue that brings healing is a tree of life,
    but a deceitful tongue crushes the spirit.
A happy heart makes the face cheerful,
    but heartache crushes the spirit.
                      Proverbs 15:1–4, 13, NIV

FULFILLING YOUR LOVE

How kind and loving You are, O God. You gave up Your heavenly kingdom and came to earth for us. When You viewed my sins, You showed Your mercy and grace by dying for me. Thank You for Your love. Thank You for living in my heart and directing me each day.

Because of Your kindness to me, I wholeheartedly give You first place in my heart. You accepted me just the way I was. Now I'm learning to love and accept others right where they are. May they feel Your love through me. Because of Your forgiving grace, I'm learning to forgive. May they seek forgiveness from You. Because I can trust You, I'm learning to be caring and trustworthy. May they, in turn, learn to trust and depend on You.

How fulfilling is Your love. I praise You for it. Your Spirit fills my being. Your endless love overflows like an artesian well. Because of this, I pass it on to others. In this way, Father, may I fulfill Your love and Your commission to spread the gospel. Amen.

I WILL BLESS YOU, LORD

No matter where I am, Lord, I can lift my heart to You in praise. Nothing or no one can interfere with our communion. Thank You for giving me the privilege of talking with You any time. It's so good to know You are always here for me. I'm not put on hold. I don't get a computerized voice. Neither are You in a bad mood nor unwilling to listen. May I always be here for You in return.

I will bless You, Lord. With my mind, my heart, my hands I offer You praise. How thankful I am for Your Holy Spirit and how You minister to me. You are so dear, so kind, so loving. How can I ever be deserving of Your love?

As I come to You, let nothing stand between this special relationship we share. If there be any malice between me and other persons, I lay it at Your altar and forgive them unconditionally. As soon as possible I will go and attempt to right the hard feelings. If there be any sin in me, I repent and ask Your forgiveness. I put my faith in You. My heart opens wide its doors. With an eager mind and bending will, I await direction from You. I long to serve You in word and deed.

I bow before You, I offer You my praise, my adoration, my love. You are a soothing balm to my soul. You give me peace, joy, caution, direction, and discipline. You give me strength and courage daily.

In my car, on the bus, in the elevator, on my job, in a meeting, in the kitchen, even at a ball game I will keep my heart tuned and bless You. In everything I do and say, I give You praise and glory.

❑❑❑

Bless the Lord, O my soul: and all that is within me, bless his holy name.
Bless the Lord, O my soul, and forget not all his benefits:
Who forgiveth all thine iniquities; who healeth all thy diseases;
Who redeemeth thy life from destruction; who crowneth thee with loving kindness and tender mercies;
Who satisfieth thy mouth with good things; so that thy youth is renewed like the eagle's.

Bless the Lord, ye his angels, that excel in strength, and do his commandments, harkening unto the voice of His word.
Bless ye the Lord, all ye his hosts; ye ministers of his, that do his pleasure.
Bless the Lord, all his works in all places of his dominion; bless the Lord, O my soul.

Psalm 103:1–7, 20–22, KJV

THROUGH LIFE'S CHANGES

Thank You, Father, for always being with me, not only now but for eternity. You were here before the earth and galaxies were formed. I marvel at how You have no beginning or end.

Life changes through the years, but You do not. You remain the same yesterday, today, and through all the tomorrows to come. Even though You never change, You perceive every season of my life. Thank You, Lord, for taking time to know everything about me and for caring for my insignificant (yet important to me) needs.

Everything that is good and perfect comes from You, O Lord and Creator. How great are Your fullness and wonder. You shine on my life day and night with no shadow of turning away. Thank You for keeping the promises You gave in Your Word. You never forsake, You never fail. You are truth, You are life.

When I go through life's changes, I sometimes find myself getting way off base. But You snatch me from destructive situations. Thank You for being here. At times I can't see why things happen the way they do. But You know, and You are still here. Thank You for being patient with me. Thank You for how Your compassion and love never fail.

I'm growing in my walk with You. Because of all You teach me, I'm learning to give my joys, my worries, my disappointments, my goals, and dreams. They are all in Your sure hands. Lord, You are first now in everything I do and plan.

What a comfort to know You will live forever and ever, and that I can always be with You. You have promised to always be my God, and keep me Your child. Through eternity, I cling to You, the Rock of my salvation. I shall never fear, for You are with me. You are first, last, always, my God and my dearest Friend.

❑❑❑

But I trusted in thee,
O Lord: I said, Thou art my God.
My times are in thy hand. . . .
Psalm 31:14–15, KJV

Take my will, and make it Thine;
It shall be no longer mine.
Take my heart—it is Thine own;
It shall be Thy royal throne.

All to Jesus now I give,
From this hour for Him to live;
While before His cross I bow,
He doth hear my humble vow.

Unknown

IN YOU I BELIEVE

Father, I look back on my life at the many things You have done for me and I am deeply grateful. Thank You for dear Christians whom You led to pray for me in times of need. Your love and their prayers have strengthened me.

Because of all You have done, I am not afraid of what may come. You have given me a spirit of power and love and self-discipline. I'm not afraid to tell others about You, for I love You and I want everyone to know of Your love. Thank You for how You saved me and for Your power that helps me live a holy life.

In all the uncertainties around me, I trust in You, I believe in You, and I know You guard all that I do.

❑❑❑

And of this gospel I was appointed
a herald and an apostle and a teacher.
That is why I am suffering as I am.
Yet I am not ashamed,
because I know whom I have believed,
and am convinced that he is able
to guard what I have
entrusted to him for that day.
2 Timothy 1:11–12, NIV

I KNOW NOT WHY GOD'S WONDROUS GRACE

I know not why God's wondrous grace
To me He hath made known,
Nor why, unworthy, Christ in love
Redeemed me for His own.

I know not how this saving faith
To me He did impart,
Nor how believing in His Word
Wrought peace within my heart.

I know not how the Spirit moves,
Convincing men of sin,
Revealing Jesus through the Word,
Creating faith in Him.

I know not when my Lord may come,
At night or noonday fair,
Nor if I'll walk the vale with Him,
Or meet Him in the air.

But "I know whom I have believed,
And am persuaded that he is able
To keep that which I've committed
Unto him against that day."

Daniel Webster Whittle

MY SOUL THIRSTS FOR YOU

Parched and worn, I come to You.
  Escaping sin and strife.
I dip my cup into Your well,
  That I may gain new life.

Repentant tears streak down my face,
  I lift my praise to You.
Thank You for Your living fount,
  For strength I gain anew.

❑❑❑

Jesus answered and said unto her,
  Whosoever drinketh of
this water shall thirst again:
  But whosoever drinketh
of the water that I shall give him
  shall never thirst;
but the water that I shall give him
  shall be in him a well of water
springing up into everlasting life.
  John 4:13–14, KJV

❑❑❑

THE ARMOR OF GOD

Finally, be strong in the Lord and in his mighty power. Put on the full armor of God so that you can take your stand against the devil's schemes. For our struggle is not against flesh and blood, but against the rulers, against the authorities, against the powers of this dark world and against the spiritual forces of evil in the heavenly realms. Therefore put on the full armor of God, so that when the day of evil comes, you may be able to stand your ground, and after you have done everything, to stand.

Ephesians 6:10–13, NIV

❑❑❑

Thank You for giving me Your armor. As I struggle with life's battles, I trust You to fight them for me.

GIRDED WITH TRUTH

At times my daily load is too heavy. Gird me with Your truth. Teach me the right words to say. Help me understand Your precepts. Fill me with Your goodness and Your loving kindness, especially when I'm treated unkindly. Thank You for being near. Your truth and mercy still endure. Your word is right and true. Great is Your faithfulness. May Your love and truth protect me.

Your word have I hidden in my heart so I might not sin, and I will be faithful to You.

167

BREASTPLATE OF RIGHTEOUSNESS

When unkind things are said and done to my face and behind my back, I praise You for Your breastplate of righteousness. Some things people say may be lies. When I'm tempted to become bitter and hateful and want to strike out, thank You for helping me. You are my defender. In You I trust. You protect me over and over against the fiery darts of the devil.

I know Your righteousness is everlasting and Your laws are true. How I delight in Your commands. You know best, my Lord. I will follow Your statutes, for they are right. You give me understanding and foresight beyond my own abilities. Thank You for how You teach me justice and compassion. I praise You for the way You remind me to stay close to what is right, not what I wish to do. I never want You to be ashamed of me. I take refuge in You, my Redeemer.

Thank You for preserving me in Your righteousness. Thank You for hearing my prayers and saving me when times are hard. I will honor and fear You even when it hurts. Because I'm obedient to You, I know You will make my way straight before me, so I may do what is just and right.

Shoes of the Gospel of Peace

Lord, Jesus, let my feet be swift and beautiful for You. Put upon them Your shoes of the gospel of peace.

Prepare me with Your Word and Your Holy Spirit so I can follow Your will throughout each day.

As I rub shoulders with those around me who feel bitterness and anger, lift me up so I'm not pulled into negative attitudes. Let sin not catch me in its heartless traps. Keep me safe, I pray.

I will not get caught in the snares of arguing and discord. Instead, I praise You for helping me to follow Your teachings, so I may have peace and joy in my heart.

When troubles surround me, I shall not fear. Though all may seem against me, I'm confident in Your ways of solving problems. Thank You for how each time You reach out and help me.

Thank You for making my feet like the deer. You enable me to stand on the heights or in the valleys. You broaden the paths beneath my feet and help my ankles be strong and not turn.

At each battle's end, my soul rests in You, O God, for You have been good to me. Thank You for Your shoes, the gospel of peace.

SHIELD OF FAITH

I will face each problem head on, trusting You, Lord, to go before me. When troubles seem frightening, I know nothing can go past Your shield as long as my heart is where You want it to be.

You are my refuge and shield. Your strength and protection cover me like feathers. Praise You, Lord, for Your faithfulness. You are my shield and my rampart, my fort and my bulwark.

Each time I face trials, I wait in hope and confidence on You. My heart rejoices in Your loving presence. I trust in Your holy name. You surround me with Your glory.

You help me hold my head high in all circumstances. When I'm faithful to You, I have no need to be ashamed. My voice cries out for You and You surround me with Your favor as a shield. Thank You for fighting my cause and for Your justice that shines through the wrong.

I will keep my covenant to obey You each day regardless of the circumstances. Only then can You find favor in me and be my shield. Praise be to You, O God, for Your shield of faith.

HELMET OF SALVATION

You, Lord, are my strength and salvation, my strong deliverer. You protect my head when the battles come. Keep my thoughts pure, I pray. Let me not even flicker a thought on wickedness. When foul talk and dirty stories float about, help me walk away so the seeds aren't planted in my mind. I will offer good remarks. My mind will stay on You. I'll share my joy and love for You with others and claim victories over sin. I'll lift Your name in praise.

Lord, thank You for granting my requests to save those from sin who curse You. Help them to turn from their wicked ways, for them to see how much You love them. You have anointed me to serve You. Thank You for answering my prayers when I come to You with a pure heart.

There may be times when there is so much stress I feel like I'm losing my mental bearings. Help me then too, dear Father. You are all-understanding, all-compassionate, all-knowing. I trust my emotional well-being to Your care. When I am weak, You are strong! I know You won't leave me. During this time, guard my thoughts and help me. Grant me the strength to shove out the grief and bad thoughts, to let them go. Help me to fix my mind on what is true and noble, right and pure, lovely and admirable, excellent and worthy of praise. Thank You for Your helmet of salvation.

Sword of the Spirit

When temptations come, dear Father, and terrible things happen, help me remember what to do. Not only will I praise You for victory to come, but I will fine-tune my whole being to obey Your will. I can't always sit back and do nothing, so I pray for guidance.

I'll take a firm stand for right. Though evil beset me, I shall not be moved from my place by Your side. I'll reach for the most aggressive piece of armor You've given me, the sword of truth.

Remind me not to run ahead of You but to await the instructions in Your Word. When I tremble with fear, I turn and see that You are beside me. I speak Your name and sense Your protecting presence.

How I marvel and praise You when I see You contend with the enemy who seeks to harm me or my loved ones. You take up the shield and buckler. In a heartbeat You come to my aid. You brandish the spear, the javelin, Your sword against those who pursue me. You are my God, my salvation. Through Your power, the wrongdoers are caught in their own snares and they fall in the very pits they have dug to destroy others.

Life's battles didn't used to be so intense. Times are worsening. It's like the forces of good and evil are warring all around us. Even those who don't profess to be Christians wonder if we are in the end times. Satan is a ravenous beast with sharp teeth eager to devour all in his path. His words are forked and cunning, ready to trip me up if I'm not alert to Your direction.

I wait. I search Your Word for direction and strength. At Your signal, You call me to arms. I claim the precious Scriptures in Your Word with fearless authority. The very mention of Your name in praise causes the devil to shrink and flee. The Lord redeems me, His lowly servant.

By Your righteous and powerful Word, the battle is won once again. Your Word is a double-edged sword in my hands. I will carry it in my heart everywhere I go and give You all the glory.

Thank You, Father, for Your sword of the Spirit, Your holy Bible.

HOW CAN I REPAY YOU?

Lord, You have done so much for me. How can I ever repay You? I want to tell everyone how loving and kind You are. When I was buried in a quicksand of sin, You rescued me and set my feet on a firm, solid foundation. That Foundation is You, Lord Jesus, the solid Rock.

You died for me and bought me with a price. After that, You sent me a Comforter to assure me of Your constant presence, Your Holy Spirit.

You are so merciful for giving me life eternal. I don't deserve Your love. I feel humbled to my knees at the very thought of Your compassion.

How can I ever repay You for all You've done? The only thing I can offer You is my worship and praise. The best I can give is a contrite heart of thanksgiving.

❏❏❏

"Has not my hand made all these things,
and so they came into being?"
declares the Lord.
"This is the one I esteem:
he who is humble and contrite in spirit,
and trembles at my word."
Isaiah 66:2, NIV

GIVE ME THY HEART

"Give me thy heart," says the Father above,
No gift so precious to Him as our love;
Softly He whispers, wherever thou art,
"Gratefully trust me and give me thy heart."

"Give me thy heart," says the Saviour of men,
Calling in mercy again and again;
"Turn now from sin, and from evil depart,
Have I not died for thee? Give me thy heart."

"Give me thy heart," says the Spirit divine,
"All that thou hast, to my keeping resign;
Grace more abounding is mind to impart,
Make full surrender and give me thy heart."

Eliza Edmunds Hewitt

ONE MORE TIME

Father, my time is short here on earth. There is still much to be done. My body grows weary, yet my drive to serve You and help others is so intense. Please let me do for You one more time that the world may be a little better.

Thank You for letting me be a servant for You.

❑❑❑

I have fought the good fight,
I have finished the race,
I have kept the faith.
Now there is in store for me
the crown of righteousness,
which the Lord, the righteous Judge,
will award to me on that day—
and not only me,
but also to all
who have longed for his appearing.
2 Timothy 4:7–8, NIV

175

Evening Prayer as Incense Sweet

Evening comes. Rest at last. I look back over my day and thank You for Your help and leading. Now at my bedside altar I lift my praise to You for Your loving kindness. Each night I look forward to meeting with You here. Like a little child arriving home from school, I curl up in Your arms and reflect on the events of the day.

Thank You for working out some problems while I listened to You. Thank You for those gentle warnings so I wouldn't err. I hope I pleased You with my actions. Forgive me for the times I slipped up.

I offer my praise to You as sweet incense. May this essence mixed with my praise ascend to Your heavenly altar. Lord Jesus, I pray for You to present me to Your Father so I may tell Him of my love.

I rest now, enveloped in Your care, and look forward to a new day with You.

❏❏❏

O Lord, I call to you; come quickly to me.
Hear my voice when I call to you.
May my prayer be set before you like incense;
may the lifting up of my hands
be like the evening sacrifice.
Psalm 141:1–2, NIV

IN EVERYTHING I PRAISE YOU

Your decisions for my life are right, O Lord, for You are my Father. You care for me. You are the Potter. Shape me as You would. Teach me Your lessons, that I may be worthy of being Your child. Help me to be pliable clay so You can form me the way You please. I have no fear of Your plan, Lord. Instead, I put my trust completely in You.

I may not understand why things happen the way they do. I may even cry out in difficult times, when I don't see the reasoning of it all. Yet I will let You purify me in Your loving way.

Make me like silver and gold as you refine me and skim away the dross and impurities. At times this is difficult, but I must trust You and obey, because You know what is best for me.

When the trials come, help me draw closer to You. I know You, Lord Jesus, suffered too. Through each struggle, I will strive to remain true. Afterward, as You have promised, I will share again the wonderful joy You have waiting for me.

I praise You in everything, Lord, that the will of God will be accomplished through me.

Be joyful always;
pray continually;
give thanks in all circumstances,
for this is God's will
for you in Christ Jesus.
1 Thessalonians 5:16–18, NIV

When you lie down, you will not be afraid;
    when you lie down, your sleep will be sweet.
Have no fear of sudden disaster
    or of the ruin that overtakes the wicked,
for the Lord will be your confidence
    and will keep your foot from being snared.
Proverbs 3:24–26, NIV

Rejoice in the Lord always. I will say it again: Rejoice! Let your gentleness be evident to all. The Lord is near. Do not be anxious about anything, but in everything, by prayer and petition, with thanksgiving present your requests to God. And the peace of God, which transcends all understanding, will guard your hearts and minds in Christ Jesus.

Philippians 4:4–7, NIV

PART 14

IN HIS NAME

WE PRAISE THEE, O GOD, OUR REDEEMER

We praise Thee, O God, our Redeemer Creator,
In grateful devotion our tribute we bring.
We lay it before Thee, we kneel and adore Thee,
We bless Thy holy name, glad praises we bring.

We worship Thee, God of our fathers,
    we bless Thee;
Through trouble and tempest our guide
    Thou hast been,
When perils o'ertake us,
    escape Thou wilt make us,
And with Thy help, O Lord, our battles we win.

With voices united our praises we offer,
To Thee, great Jehovah, glad anthems we raise.
Thy strong arm will guide us,
    our God is beside us;
To Thee, our great Redeemer, forever be praise.
Amen.

Julia Buckley Cady Cory

A PSALM OF DAVID

O Lord our Lord, how excellent is thy name
    in all the earth! who hast set thy glory above
    the heavens.
When I consider thy heavens, the works of thy
    fingers, the moon and stars which thou hast
    ordained;
What is man, that thou art mindful of him?
    and the son of man, that thou visitest him?
For thou has made him a little lower than the
    angels, and hast crowned him with glory
    and honour.
Thou madest him to have dominion over the
    works of thy hands; thou has put
    all things under his feet:
O Lord our Lord, how excellent is thy name
    in all the earth!

Psalm 8:1, 3–6, 9, KJV

WONDERFUL

Wonderful You are who made me.
Wonderful You are who knows me.
Wonderful You are who called me.
Wonderful You are who forgave me.
Wonderful You are who saved me.
Wonderful You are who leads me.
Wonderful is Your name.

❏❏❏

For unto us a child is born,
unto us a son is given;
and the government shall be upon his shoulder;
and his name shall be called Wonderful, Counselor,
The mighty God, The everlasting Father,
The Prince of Peace.
Isaiah 9:6, KJV

❏❏❏

For the Lord gives wisdom,
and from his mouth come knowledge and
understanding.
He holds victory in store for the upright,
he is a shield to those whose walk is
blameless,
for he guards the course of the just
and protects the way of his faithful ones.

Then you will understand what is right and just
and fair—every good path.
For wisdom will enter your heart,
and knowledge will be pleasant to your soul.
Proverbs 2:6–10, NIV

181

COUNSELOR

You are my Counselor, Father. You are the one I can turn to for guidance. I trust in You completely and Your almighty wisdom. Without You my own reasoning is finite and insecure. When I need to know Your will, I can ask of You and You find ways to guide me. I open my heart. I read Your Word and pray. You are there to give me a bountiful supply of wisdom.

You, my Counselor, are wiser than all and stronger than any living being. How foolish and shameful the ideas of this world are in light of Your divine greatness. You alone are wisdom and glory. I can never brag of my own accomplishments. My real success is through You.

Your direction unfolds before me. You lay out the course so simply. Yet I must be obedient and in tune with Your will to understand. I read Your Word and store its lessons in my heart so I can remember the right paths. Over and over I repeat Scriptures in my thoughts.

All who know You speak in reverence of Your name. They marvel at Your glorious foresight and counsel. You alone give abundant life and right decisions. Because of this, I experience indescribable joy!

You, Father, are Light. In You there is no darkness. Long ago You said, "Let there be light."

I'm beginning to understand that light comes from the pure brightness of Your glorious presence. Once I lived in darkness and sin, but now I follow You, my Guide, my Counselor. Let me continue in

Your paths that I may always experience joy and fellowship with other believers and with You, my God.

Thank You for giving me eternal life through Your Son, Jesus Christ. When I err, tend me, prune me as a vine, so I may grow stronger and more useful for Your service.

I praise You, my Lord and Counselor, and lift Your name on high forever.

MIGHTY GOD

You are so great, O Mighty God. There is no other like You. I praise You with all my heart and soul. All You are and all You create shows splendor and majesty. You unfold the morning skies like a holy robe. You furl it again through the universe at evening to expose the vast starlit heavens. The waters reflect Your glorious rays.

I stretch out on the grass and gaze at the clouds as they play tag like huge, animated animals. The wind blows as though Your forceful breath pushes each cloud with huge gusts. Thunder and lightning put on a dramatic display like a vigorous chariot race.

You, Mighty God, created the mountains in all their grandeur, once covered with gushing waters. At Your command the waters left and formed rivers in the valleys below. Geysers shoot up, mountains tremble, mud and lava fill once-clear rivers. Some waters even go dry. It all is so fearful. The very balance of nature is threatened, but You have control. Through it all, the Earth is purged of disease. The mountains have bellowed out ash that feeds our soil. New green sprouts and lush grass grow. The animals and people return, and life begins anew.

In the same way You shook my life and cleansed me of impurities. Little by little You created new growth in me that is fresh and pleasing to You.

How can the birds know where to make such perfect nests? How do they know where to migrate? You planned it for them, mighty God. How amazing! How wonderful! You provide creeks and ponds in pastures for the animals. The cattle come out by day, the wild animals by night to drink.

You give us grains, vegetables, and fruits that seed and reseed themselves. You even planned seasons so all can rest through the winter. In spring nature awakens and new life begins.

How important are Your works, O Lord. In Your wisdom You have made each one. I will sing praise to Your name. I will meditate on Your good works and rejoice in Your great love.

Rejoice, O my soul. Let all that is within me praise the Almighty God.

❑❑❑

For great is the Lord and
most worthy of praise. . . .
Psalm 96:4, NIV

I SING OF THE ALMIGHTY POWER OF GOD

I sing the almighty power of God,
That made the mountains rise;
That spread the flowing seas abroad,
And built the lofty skies.
I sing the wisdom that ordained
The sun to rule the day;
The moon shines full at His command,
And all the stars obey.

I sing the goodness of the Lord,
That filled the earth with food;
He formed the creatures with His word,
And pronounced them good.
Lord, how Thy wonders are displayed,
Where'er I turn my eye;
If I survey the ground I tread,
O gaze upon the sky!

There's not a plant or flower below,
But makes Thy glories known;
And clouds arise, and tempests blow,
By order from Thy throne;
While all that borrows life from Thee
Is ever in Thy care
And everywhere that man can be,
Thou, God, are present there. Amen.

Isaac Watts

A VOICE OF ONE CALLING

"In the desert prepare the way for the Lord;
    make straight in the wilderness
    a highway for our God.
Every valley shall be raised up,
    every mountain and hill made low;
the rough ground shall become level,
    the rugged places a plain.
And the glory of the Lord will be revealed,
    and all mankind together will see it.
For the mouth of the Lord has spoken."
                  Isaiah 40:3–5, NIV

EVERLASTING FATHER

What a loving Father You are, my God. Because we couldn't comprehend Your love, You showed us what kind of a Father You are by sending us Your Son.

I bow before You in reverence and fear. The only way I can approach Your throne is through Your Son, Jesus Christ. He has taken away my sins by shedding His priceless blood. This way You can look upon me, Your unworthy child.

Thank You for loving me. From You, came my very being. In You, is my course of life. You know my needs, my abilities, my longings. You listen to my joys, my sadness, my frustrations, my dreams. You are my everlasting Father. Thank You for always being present with me. When I call on Your name, I praise You for already being here.

□□□

God said to Moses, "I am who I am. This is what you are to say to the Israelites: 'I AM has sent me to you.'"

God also said to Moses, "Say to the Israelites, 'The Lord, the God of your fathers—God of Abraham, the God of Isaac and the God of Jacob—has sent me to you.' This is my name forever, the name by which I am to be remembered from generation to generation."

Exodus 3:14–15, NIV

PRINCE OF PEACE

Praise You for peace, Lord. Not the uncertain peace the world offers, but a peace of heart and mind that only comes from knowing You, the Prince of Peace.

May the rich exalt You and put You first. May the needy lift You up in praise. May all experience true peace and the fullness of life with You as Savior and Lord.

Thank You for Your tender care. Your compassion never fails. During the happy times, may Your guiding presence and peace be acknowledged. In the sad times of want, sickness, or death, still may Your comfort and peace be felt.

Although we are of the world, thank You for Your power to overcome life's overwhelming problems. What a precious gift, Your love and peace. It isn't fragile or fluffy or temporary as the world gives, but deep, satisfying, and dependable, because it comes from You, Almighty God. You are the Prince of Peace. The greatness of its source is more than our finite minds can comprehend.

In all circumstances, I shall not be troubled or afraid. I believe in the Father and I believe in You, my Prince of Peace. I praise You, Lord, with all my heart, mind and soul. No matter what happens, I accept Your peace and I will put my trust in You.

Peace I leave with you, my peace I give unto you: not as the world giveth, give I unto you. Let not your heart be troubled, neither let it be afraid.

John 14:27, KJV

This is what the Sovereign Lord, the Holy One of Israel, says:

"In repentance and rest is your salvation,
in quietness and trust is your strength. . . ."
Isaiah 30:15, NIV

EMMANUEL, GOD WITH US

Emmanuel, I praise You for promising me You will never leave me nor forsake me. You are my Father, my Helper, my Guide. I shall never fear, for I know You are with me. Thank You for protecting me wherever I am, day and night.

You fill me with strength and courage. When troubles come, others may flee, but You stand by me: my dearest Friend, my Savior.

I praise You for being with me always, even through the end of my earthly life. You, Lord, are the One who died for my sin, yet You live forevermore.

Thank You for always being with me and letting me be with You. Thank You for Your wonderful peace that passes all understanding.

190

Then Jesus came to them and said, "All authority in heaven and on earth has been given to me. Therefore go and make disciples of all nations, baptizing them in the name of the Father and of the Son and of the Holy Spirit, and teaching them to obey everything I have commanded you. And surely I am with you always, to the very end of the age."

Matthew 28:18–20, NIV

JEHOVAH

Jehovah, I give You honor and glory. I trust You with my life. I can always depend on You. Thank You for Your unfailing love. You are trustworthy and sure. In every situation Your promises are sure. You are truth and righteousness. In You, there is no fault.

How virtuous are Your ways. Your laws and directions are upright and perfect. In You, I rely and place all my confidence. You are my King, bold and sure. Your faithfulness and love never sway.

Thank You for Your care. Praise be to You, Jehovah, Most High, my God, my Savior.

That men may know that thou,
whose name alone is JEHOVAH,
art the most high over all the earth.
Psalm 83:18, KJV

GUIDE ME, O THOU GREAT JEHOVAH

Guide me, O Thou great Jehovah;
Pilgrim through this barren land;
I am weak, but Thou art mighty,
Hold me with Thy powerful hand;

Bread of heaven, Bread of heaven,
Feed me till I want no more,
Feed me till I want no more.

William Williams

CREATOR

Praise be to You, O God, my Creator, the source of my entire existence. You were here in the beginning. You were present when there was nothing—no form, only darkness. At Your mighty command there was light. It must have been quite a sight to view the streaks of light shooting across the darkness, dividing nothingness into timely submission. Thank You for how You put light into my life, dispelling darkness and sin.

You created water and land, the sun, moon, and stars. You made creatures of all kinds. Wisdom and balance are rolled from Your fingertips. Then You created man and woman. Some of Your creation gives You joy. Others cause grief. How I pray to reflect You and give You joy, gladness, and pride for having me as Your child.

Your Word says when You completed Your creation, You looked at it and said it was good. May I always make You feel pleased that You created me, Lord. May I spend my life giving honor and glory to You.

Praise be to You, O God, my Creator.

In the beginning God created the heaven and the earth. And the earth was without form, and void; and darkness was upon the face of the deep. And the Spirit of God moved upon the face of the waters. And God said, Let there be light: and there was light.

And God said, Let the waters under the heaven be gathered together unto one place, and let the dry land appear: and it was so.

And God said, Let the earth bring forth grass, the herb yielding seed, and the fruit tree yielding fruit after his kind, whose seed is in itself, upon the earth: and it was so.

And God made two great lights: the greater light to rule the day, and the lesser light to rule the night: he made the stars also.

And God created great whales, and every living creature that moveth. . . . And God saw that it was good.

And God said, Let us make man in our image, after our likeness. . . . So God created man in his own image, in the image of God created he him; male and female created he them.

And God saw everything that he had made, and, behold, it was very good. And the evening and the morning were the sixth day.

Genesis 1:1–3, 9, 11, 16, 21, 26–27, 31, KJV

MASTER

You, Lord, are
    my Master
    my Commander
    my Governor and Guide
    my Teacher
    Head of our home.

Teach me, Master,
    to follow
    to serve
    to labor
    to endure
    to trust.

I bow before You,
Master, in obedience and praise.
May I live so You can someday say to me,
"Well done, good and faithful servant!"

No man can serve two masters:
for either he will hate the one,
and love the other;
or else he will hold to the one,
and despise the other.
Ye cannot serve God and mammon.

The disciple is not above his master,
nor the servant above his lord.

And, behold, one came and said unto him,
"Good Master, what good thing shall I do,
that I may have eternal life?
And he said unto him, "Why callest thou me good?
there is none good but one, that is, God:
but if thou wilt enter into life,
keep the commandments."

. . . "Thou shalt love the Lord thy God
with all thy heart,
and with all thy soul,
and with all thy mind. . . .
Thou shalt love thy neighbour as thyself."
Matthew 6:25; 10:24; 19:16–17; 22:37, 39, KJV

And he was in the hinder part of the ship,
asleep on a pillow:
and they awake him, and say unto him,
Master, carest thou not that we perish?
And he arose, and rebuked the wind,
and said unto the sea, Peace, be still.
And the wind ceased and there was a great calm.
And he said unto them,
Why are ye so fearful?
how is it that ye have no faith?
Mark 4:38–40, KJV

SAVIOR

Lord, You are my Savior, my Rescuer, Deliverer. Words seem inadequate to praise You for how You saved me from my sins.

How was it possible for You to be born as a man and yet still be the Son of God? You are greater than the angels. You extend Your Father's love to earth and glorify His name. What love You showed when You gave up Your glory in Heaven long enough to become a poor child, growing up, loving and serving, and finally laying down Your life. While You lived on earth, You didn't even have a pillow to put Your head on.

All You did for us made it possible for me to have a joyful abundant life through You. Thank You for being my Savior and for allowing me to be Your servant.

Who being in the form of God,
thought it not robbery to be equal with God:
But made himself of no reputation,
and took upon him the form of a servant,
and was made in the likeness of men:
And being found in fashion as a man,
he humbled himself,
and became obedient unto death,
even the death of the cross.
Wherefore God also hath highly exalted him and
given him a name which is above every name:
That at the name of Jesus every knee should bow,
of things in heaven, and things in earth,
and things under the earth;
And that every tongue should confess
that Jesus Christ is Lord,
to the glory of God the Father.
Philippians 2:6–11, KJV

Arise my soul, arise, shake off thy guilty fears,
The bleeding sacrifice, in my behalf appears.
Before the throne my surety stands,
My name is written on His hands.

He ever lives above, for me to intercede,
His all redeeming love, His precious blood to plead,
His blood atoned for all our race
And sprinkles now the throne of grace.

Five bleeding wounds He bears, received
    on Calvary,
They pour effectual prayers, and strongly
    plead for me.
"For him, oh forgive," they cry,
"Nor let that ransomed sinner die."

The Father hears Him pray, His dear anointed One,
He cannot turn away the presence of His Son.
His Spirit answers to the Blood,
And tells me, I am born of God.

Charles Wesley

REDEEMER

Praise be to You, my Redeemer. How mighty You are, the Savior of all who give You their hearts. You alone are able to keep me from slipping into sin and wrong. Each time I confront temptation's engulfing power, You rescue me by Your victorious strength. Each time You fight life's battles between good and evil for me. How thankful I am that I don't have to fight them by myself. I simply obey as You go before me.

I have no fear of judgment, for You are there, already lovingly interceding on my behalf. All I had to do was open my heart's door and let You in. When I repented of my sins, You cast them as far off as the east is from the west, to be forgotten and never to return.

Nothing can ever keep me from You, my Lord, my Redeemer. Not life nor death. The angels will not, and the powers of hell cannot. Any fears for today or the future can't keep me from You. No matter where I should need to go, beneath the ocean or above the stars, You are with me and I with You.

Thank You for redeeming me and giving me life anew.

❑❑❑

Yet their Redeemer is strong;
the Lord Almighty is his name.
He will vigorously defend their cause. . . .
Jeremiah 50:34, NIV

LAMB OF GOD

If I could gaze into the heavens and get one tiny glimpse of You on Your throne, I imagine I would behold a royal King, sitting by His holy Father. I would love to see Your eyes. I think they would be filled with authority, yet tender love and understanding. The very thought of this surges strength to my being and adds zest and enthusiasm to all I do. May everything I say and do bring honor to You.

In all Your purity, I behold You, Lord. I praise You for sacrificing Yourself for me. Your blood spilled. No other blood needs to be shed to redeem me. The only offering I can give You, my Savior, is my life, filled with praise and honor. You laid down Your life for me, now I live mine for You.

You never complained, O Lamb of God, when You were mistreated, beaten, spat upon. I'm overwhelmed with love to think how You willingly went to the cross like a lamb about to be slain. You made no attempt to defend Yourself.

How was it possible for You to pay my ransom and rescue me from the devil himself? Praise You, O Lord, for spilling Your pure, cleansing blood for me.

All my days I have this hope and ambition: to serve You, to tell all who will listen of the unlimited joy You have given me.

You are worthy of praise, O Lamb of God. You are worthy to receive glory and honor and riches and strength and power and blessing forever.

GRACE ALONE

Not saved are we by trying,
from self can come no aid;
'Tis on the blood relying,
once for our ransom paid.

'Tis looking unto Jesus,
the holy one and just;
'Tis His grace that saves—
it is not "try" but "trust!"

Anonymous

❑❑❑

The next day John saw Jesus coming toward him
and said, "Look, the Lamb of God,
who takes away the sin of the world!
This is the one I meant when I said,
'A man who comes after me has surpassed me
because he was before me,'
I myself did not know him,
but the reason I came baptizing with water
was that he might be revealed to Israel."
John 1:29–31, NIV

202

But John tried to deter him, saying,
"I need to be baptized by you,
and do you come to me?"
Jesus replied,
"Let it be so now,
it is proper for us to do this
to fulfill all righteousness."
Then John consented.
As soon as Jesus was baptized,
he went up out of the water.
At that moment heaven was opened,
and he saw the Spirit of God descending
like a dove and lighting on him.
And a voice from heaven said,
"This is my Son, whom I love;
with him I am well pleased."
Matthew 3:14–17, NIV

Come, let us join our cheerful songs
With angels round the throne;
Ten thousand thousand are their tongues,
But all their joys are one.

"Worthy the Lamb that died," they cry,
"To be exalted thus."
"Worthy is the Lamb," our lips reply,
"For He was slain for us."

The whole creation joins as one
To bless the sacred Name
Of Him that sits upon the throne,
And to adore the Lamb.

Isaac Watts

BRIGHT AND MORNING STAR

In this evil world, I turn to You, my Bright and Morning
Star. I will not fear the sinful darkness that lurks about
me, for You, Lord, are there lighting my way.

Once You left in clouds of glory. I look forward to
Your return, in all Your brightness and glory.

❑❑❑

"I, Jesus, have sent my angel to give you this testimony
for the churches. I am the Root and the Offspring of
David, and the bright Morning Star."

Revelation 22:16, NIV

COMFORTER

Thank You, Father, for Your Holy Spirit, Your Comforter. What peace it gives me to know You are with me throughout my day. The world can't see Your comfort unless they choose to accept Jesus Christ as their Savior. Otherwise, they can never recognize Your sustaining power and grace.

I have so many questions to ask You about things I can't understand. I realize some answers may not come until I see You face to face. This is where I learn to trust You and depend upon Your Word. Guide me into truth and knowledge, so I can make right decisions. Let me learn from Your stories of old so I may grow in You.

I wonder what it was like that evening long ago when Your disciples hid in fear behind bolted doors, not knowing what to do next. Would I have been so fearful? I think so.

Past the bolted doors You came and stood before them. "Peace be with You!" You assured them.

I would have been thrilled and frightened at the same time if I could have seen Your hands and feet and side.

"Peace be with you," again You charged. "As the Father has sent me, so send I you." You breathed on them, and they received Your Comforter, Your Holy Spirit!

Breathe on me now, I pray. Fill me with Your Spirit. Grant me Your Comforter. Give me Your power so I may share the gospel in my life to everyone around me.

Thank You, Lord, for Your Comforter.

If ye know me, keep my commandments.
And I will pray the Father,
and he shall give you another Comforter,
that he may abide with you forever;
Even the Spirit of truth;
whom the world cannot receive,
because it seeth him not,
neither knoweth him: but ye know him;
for he dwelleth with you, and shall be in you.
I will not leave you comfortless:
I will come to you.
But the Comforter, which is the Holy Ghost,
whom the Father will send in my name,
he shall teach you all things,
and bring all things to your remembrance,
whatsoever I have said unto you.
John 14:15–18, 26, KJV

LIGHT OF THE WORLD

A world lost in darkness
No light could they see;
A ray came from Jesus
To save one like me

A brightness like noonday,
Shone down from above;
God's beam lit my pathway,
With Jesus' pure love.

Do you live in the shadows,
Discouraged and lost?
See the light from the Savior.
He paid the cost.

❑❑❑

When Jesus spoke again to the people, he said,
"I am the light of the world.
Whoever follows me will never walk in darkness,
but will have the light of life."
John 8:12, NIV

THE WAY, THE TRUTH, THE LIFE

At times, Father, my ways haven't been Your ways. After I strayed from Your path, I slipped and fell, soon realizing what disaster I'd gotten myself into. Then with Your help, I struggled to faltering feet and got back on the right course. Then You gave me direction and sound judgment. Thank You for being my Way.

You gave me Your Word. In it You show me truth, and through Your truth I've been set free. Day by day I study Your Scriptures. Your Word helps me know right from wrong. Through Your Holy Spirit, it advises me in making wise decisions. It cautions me against sinful traps. Thank You for being my Truth.

Because of Your certain way and guiding truth, You lead me into joyous, abundant life. When circumstances are difficult and unsure, I still have a deep inward joy filled with victory only You can provide. Not only do I experience a victorious life here on earth, I look forward to life eternal with You in heaven. Thank You, Lord, for my life.

❑❑❑

Jesus saith unto him,
I am the way, the truth, and the life:
no man cometh unto the Father,
but by me.
John 14:6, KJV

Anywhere with Jesus

I'll go anywhere, my Savior,
If Thou wilt make it clear,
I will tell salvation's story
To lost ones far and near.

Anywhere, my Savior,
Anywhere with Thee,
Anywhere and ev'rywhere,
As Thou leadest me.

John R. Clements

Lead me in thy truth, and teach me:
for thou art the God of my salvation;
on thee do I wait all the day.
Psalm 25:5, KJV

209

GUIDE

Be Thou my guide,
Through life's treacherous way.
Be Thou my rock,
On it will I stay.

Be Thou my might;
Grant me strength anew.
Be Thou my map;
Gently lead me through.

Be Thou my song,
So I will not fear.
Be Thou my stay;
Keep me safe and near.

Be Thou my grace;
Firmly clasp my hand.
Be Thou my guide,
To the promised land.

THE POTTER

Lord, it makes no difference what comes my way. What really matters is for me to be within Your will. Help me become soft and pliable so You can mold me the way You know I should be.

The potter's wheel spins 'round and 'round. Gentle fingers form the soft clay into the master's desired creation. To the potter, there is purpose in each turn.

At times my life seems to be spinning. Slow me down, Lord. You are the Potter of my life. Let me heed to Your molding so I can be a product of Your perfect plan.

❑❑❑

Does not the potter have the right
to make out of the same lump of clay
some pottery for noble purposes and
some for common use?
Romans 9:21, NIV

Have Thine Own Way, Lord

Have Thine own way, Lord!
Have Thine own way!
Thou are the potter;
I am the clay.

Mold me and make me
After Thy will,
While I am waiting,
Yielded and still.

Adelaide Addison Pollard

King of Kings

You are my King of Kings, dear Lord. Your kingdom shall never end. You shall reign forever and ever.

I thank You for including me in Your kingdom. What a priceless gift You have given all those who believe in You. May You show the way for all nations. Earthly kingdoms and governments will crumble but Your kingdom, O Lord, shall ever stand.

I want to glorify You, Lord. In all my ways I will reflect Your love. The devil may roar like a lion. Sickness may seek to destroy. Death may take my body. Yet none shall win, for I am of You. Your kingdom is everlasting and lives within my heart.

All you have made will praise you, O Lord;
    your saints will extol you.
They will tell of the glory of your kingdom
    and speak of your might,
so that all men may know of your mighty acts
    and the glorious splendor of your kingdom.
Your kingdom is an everlasting kingdom,
    and your dominion endures through all
    generations.

                                    Psalm 145:10–13, NIV

PRAYER REQUESTS

_____

_____

_____

_____

_____

_____

_____

_____

_____

_____

_____

_____

_____

_____

_____

_____

_____

_____

ANSWERS TO PRAYER

_____

_____

_____

_____

_____

_____

_____

_____

_____

_____

_____

_____

_____

_____

_____

_____

_____

_____

_____

_____

_____

_____

PRAYER REQUESTS

ANSWERS TO PRAYER

_____

_____

_____

_____

_____

_____

_____

_____

_____

_____

_____

_____

_____

_____

_____

_____

_____

_____

_____

_____

_____

_____

PRAYER REQUESTS

_____

_____

_____

_____

_____

_____

_____

_____

_____

_____

_____

_____

_____

_____

_____

_____

_____

_____

_____

_____

ANSWERS TO PRAYER

_____

_____

_____

_____

_____

_____

_____

_____

_____

_____

_____

_____

_____

_____

_____

_____

_____

_____

_____

_____

_____

PRAYER REQUESTS

_____
_____
_____
_____
_____
_____
_____
_____
_____
_____
_____
_____
_____
_____
_____
_____
_____
_____
_____
_____
_____

ANSWERS TO PRAYER

_____

_____

_____

_____

_____

_____

_____

_____

_____

_____

_____

_____

_____

_____

_____

_____

_____

_____

_____

_____

_____

Anita Corrine Donihue and her pastor husband, Bob, have been serving Christ for four decades. She co-authored two gift books, *Apples for a Teacher* and *Joy to the World,* with well-known Christian author, Colleen L. Reece. Anita's work has also been featured in *Focus on the Family* and other magazines. She is a mother of five sons and grandmother of six grandchildren. Her life of serving others continually sends her to the Scriptures for guidance. *When I'm on My Knees* came from intensive prayer and study.

OTHER BOOKS BY
ANITA CORRINE DONIHUE

If you enjoyed *When I'm on My Knees,* be sure to look for these other books by Anita Corrine Donihue at your local Christian bookstore:

When I Hear His Call
The most recent book in the series addresses the issues of obedience to God's call.
    ISBN 1-58660-279-9. . . . . $4.97

When I'm Praising God
Anita's sequel to *When I'm on My Knees,* promoting praise as the key to a fulfilling Christian life.
    ISBN 1-57748-447-9. . . . . $4.97

When I'm in His Presence
Anita's third book, encouraging women to look for God's working in their everyday lives.
    ISBN 1-57748-665-X $4.97

When God Sees Me Through
Anita's fourth book in the series, celebrating the Lord's faithfulness through every circumstance of our lives.
    ISBN 1-57748-977-2. . . . . $4.97

ALSO AVAILABLE:
When I'm on My Knees Prayer Journal
Favorite selections from *When I'm on My Knees,* plus ample journaling space for your prayer requests and praise notes.
    ISBN 1-57748-836-9. . . . . $4.97

Available wherever books are sold.
Or order from:

Barbour Publishing, Inc.
P.O. Box 719
Uhrichsville, OH 44683
http://www.barbourbooks.com

If you order by mail, add $2.00 to your order for shipping.
Prices are subject to change without notice.